PUFFIN BOOKS

Edited by Eleanor Graham

PS117

GOING INTO THE PAST

No time machine is needed to take you back into the past if you have this book as your guide. Ancient man left plenty of clues if you know where to look for them and what to make of them when you have found them. Most people must have seen at some time traces of how he lived and the kind of things he did, without knowing what lay before them; and some of his works are natural features of the English landscape and stand out against the sky for anyone to see. Dr Copley shows you how to discover them for yourself, where to look, and how to recognize the evidence and understand the story which lies behind it. Parts of such work lie out of doors, working with pick and shovel, trowel and camel-hair brush. A good deal of work is also done today by aerial photography. To supplement all else there are the museums, especially local ones, and there are notes on these at the end of each section of the book. It is fully illustrated with drawings, maps, and photographs, and is recommended for all who are just beginning to be interested in the subject of archaeology, whether child or adult.

D1332026

GORDON J. COPLEY

GOING INTO THE PAST

PENGUIN BOOKS

Penguin Books Ltd, Harmondsworth, Middlesex
U.S.A.: Penguin Books Inc., 3300 Clipper Mill Road, Baltimore 11, Md
AUSTRALIA: Penguin Books Pty Ltd, 762 Whitehorse Road,
Mitcham, Victoria

—

First published by Phoenix House 1955
Published in Puffin Books 1958

To M. J. C.

Made and printed in Great Britain
by R. & R. Clark Ltd
Edinburgh

Contents

List of Plates

List of Maps

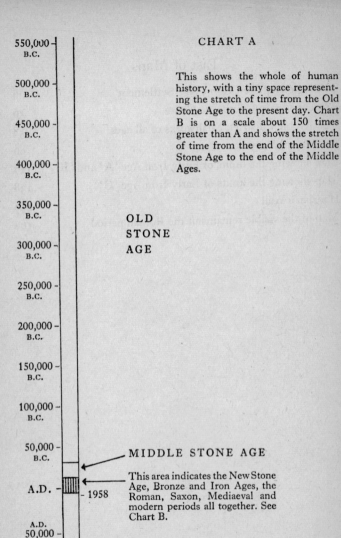

550,000 B.C.

500,000 B.C.

450,000 B.C.

400,000 B.C.

350,000 B.C.

300,000 B.C.

250,000 B.C.

200,000 B.C.

150,000 B.C.

100,000 B.C.

50,000 B.C.

A.D. —

A.D. 50,000 —

OLD STONE AGE

This shows the whole of human history, with a tiny space representing the stretch of time from the Old Stone Age to the present day. Chart B is on a scale about 150 times greater than A and shows the stretch of time from the end of the Middle Stone Age to the end of the Middle Ages.

MIDDLE STONE AGE

— 1958

This area indicates the New Stone Age, Bronze and Iron Ages, the Roman, Saxon, Mediaeval and modern periods all together. See Chart B.

2500 B.C.		New Stone Age tribes begin to arrive in Britain	↑ NEW STONE AGE
2000 B.C.		Climate becomes drier and warmer	
	1850 B.C. –	Beaker invasions begin	↓↑
		Food Vessel tribes	EARLY
		Wessex culture begins	BRONZE
1500 B.C.			AGE
		Rise of the Urn people	↓↑
			MIDDLE BRONZE
1000 B.C.		Coming of the first ploughmen	AGE ↓↑
	750 B.C. –	Deverel-Rimbury tribes arrive Climate becomes wetter and cooler	LATE BRONZE
500 B.C.			AGE ↓↑
	450 B.C. –	Invasions by Iron Age 'A' people	
	250 B.C. –	Invasions by Iron Age 'B' people	IRON AGE
	75 B.C. – 50 B.C. –	Belgic (Iron Age 'C') invasions	↓↑
A.D.	A.D. 43 –	Roman conquest begins	ROMAN
		Climate becomes a little warmer and drier	PERIOD
	A.D. 425 – A.D. 450 –	End of Roman occupation Beginning of settlement by the English tribes	↓↑
A.D. 500			
	A.D. 600 –	The English begin to accept Christianity	DARK
	A.D. 800 –	Viking raids begin	AGES
A.D. 1000			↓
	A.D. 1066 –	Norman Conquest	↑
			MIDDLE
	A.D. 1492 –	Columbus discovers the New World	AGES ↓

The Detection of Ancient Things

In one of H. G. Wells's most exciting short stories, called *The Time Machine*, he tells of an invention that made it possible to go backwards or forwards in time, just as we can travel on land from town to town or from continent to continent. Seated on his marvellous machine the 'driver' could whisk himself forward to A.D. 2000 or 5000, or backwards to the days of Julius Caesar. Once there, it was possible to march with the Roman legions in one of the invasions of southern Britain; or five hundred years later, if the machine was so adjusted, he could have come ashore with Hengist and Horsa on the coast of Kent.

When Wells wrote the story in 1895, scarcely anything was known about the many peoples who had lived in Britain before about A.D. 700. Until then the art of writing was unknown in Britain except by the Romans, and they have left only a little behind them in writing to tell us about the people they conquered and ruled for nearly four hundred years. Of all the other peoples before and immediately after them we can learn almost nothing from written history. But in the last fifty years, with the help of pick and shovel, trowel and camel-hair brush, and more recently through aerial photography, we have come to know a surprising amount about the many ancient peoples who left nothing for us in writing to describe how they lived and where they originally came from.

Even what we know now is only a tiny fragment of all we should like to know. But almost every day a little more is discovered about the distant past, and we are beginning to acquire a dim but trustworthy picture of ancient times.

The work of discovering the past is called 'archaeology', which is made up of two Greek words meaning, when taken together, the study of ancient things. This work is done largely by digging up ancient sites, that is, by 'excavating', and afterwards studying the objects and structures that are revealed by digging. Yet other valuable work is done by studying ancient sites from what may be seen and picked up on the surface of the ground; and this book is mostly concerned with such work. But before anyone can engage in field archaeology he must learn all he can about the distant past, and in the following chapters I have tried to give a short account of the main facts known to us about each period. (See Time Charts, pp. 10, 11.)

In most chapters will be found short lists of the earthworks that you may visit, so that you may, if you are fortunate, be the first to recognize other similar ones. In the photographic illustrations you will find examples of most of the kinds of earthworks that you are likely to come across, but none of the plates can give a complete representation. Each earthwork would require dozens of illustrations to make this possible. Photographs from the air can give a full plan of a site, and you should consult books from your public library which contain these aerial views. The line illustrations give plans of some important sites, but their main purpose is to give you some idea of the small finds that are constantly being made all over the country. There are also several maps and diagrams indicating the regions in which objects of certain periods are most likely to be found, and two maps, one of the Avebury district and the other of a part of Cranborne Chase, where ancient sites of all ages are especially common.

The excavation of sites is a highly skilled job, and a very expensive one to do properly. There are altogether so many ancient sites in Britain that only a very few of them will be fully understood by excavation during our lifetime. But there is much of value that may be learned from some of them by field archaeology even before they are excavated.*

When the archaeologist has done his part of the work, either by excavation, or by field work, the prehistorian can make use of the new facts so discovered, and he can add a little more to the story of the distant past. Those who write prehistory are concerned with the times before man began to write down anything about himself, and for an understanding of those times we have to depend on the study of the things he made: his household goods, the tools of his trade, his hunting gear, and his weapons of war, the things he used as jewels and to decorate his clothes or body, his tombs and his temples. The historian, on the other hand, has written or printed accounts of the past as the raw material from which he constructs the story of the less distant past; yet even he is gaining new information from the work of archaeologists; for old written accounts, and, later, printed ones, often leave out much of what we would like to know, especially concerning the everyday lives of ordinary men and women.

Archaeology, therefore, can tell us much even about historical times, and it is likely that archaeologists in A.D. 3000 will find some problems to be solved about this present age, for there are, no doubt, some everyday things, very familiar to you and me, which are not mentioned in newspapers or books, and which will only be rediscovered by digging.

Nowadays there are few young people who do not travel,

* In archaeology you will often come across the word 'culture', used to describe a group of people who are named after their chief architectural remains or tools or utensils (e.g. the Beaker Folk); or after the place where they were first found (e.g. the Windmill Hill people): or after sites where they were the only occupants or were very numerous. The Grooved-Ware culture means, for instance, a group of people who made this particular sort of pottery.

at least once a year, through the English countryside. Probably many times in your wanderings you have passed by without knowing it some of the works of ancient man. Few people, including grown-ups, recognize these things as ancient, and very few indeed have the least idea of their purpose.

In the following chapters I want to explain to you what these things are or were, and what kind of people made them; so that for many of you, 'going into the past' will become a very exciting detective adventure. When your knowledge of the distant past has increased enough you may easily make discoveries of your own. And there are still plenty of discoveries waiting to be made in every part of the country, though some parts are more promising than others. But wherever you live you are within reach, at any rate by cycle, of some of the kinds of earthworks or buildings described in this book.

All that is necessary in order to set up as a detective of ancient things is to find out just how to locate earthworks and ruined buildings, and then to learn to recognize them when you see them. Later on, when you have gathered experience 'in the field' you may, if you are keen enough, add new facts to those already known. In the last chapter I shall tell you what you can do besides simply looking at ancient sites. Without a great deal of experience you must not dig into them; but there are usually finds, such as flints and fragments of pottery, to be picked up on the surface when you know what to look for and how to look for it. In older towns much is constantly turning up, and your sharp eye may well notice something interesting when, for instance, pipes are being repaired under the street, or the foundations of new houses are being dug.

When the weather is bad there are museums to be visited; for looking at other people's finds, especially when they have been carefully classified, arranged, and described, is a great help in identifying your own discoveries. And the public library is sure to have some books of interest on the subject. Lastly there are maps. From the best of these all kinds of pleasant excursions into the past may be made if only you know how to read them; I shall do what I can to make that easier for you.

1: The Stone Ages

MAN first appeared in Britain roughly 550,000 years ago, while it was still joined to the mainland of Europe and before the English Channel came into being and made Britain an island. In those far-distant times Scotland and Ireland were covered by a vast ice-sheet like that which covers the lands round the South Pole to-day.

Hunters and Fishermen

The earliest men, and those who followed them for long after, left nothing for us to find except their tools of chipped stone or, much more rarely, of bone or antler. There is nothing in Britain to compare with the wonderful cave paintings of France and Spain. The most that we can show in the way of Old Stone Age art is a few scratches on a bone that look like the figure of a man.

For about 500,000 years, that is, for most of the time that man is known to have existed, progress was very, very slow. The tools of 100,000 years ago are not greatly different from those of 10,000 years ago. But gradually, so gradually that no man could have noticed the change, the climate became warmer, and the great sheet of ice melted and shrank and moved back ever farther towards the north. As the edge of the ice retreated so did the cold-loving animals – mammoth, reindeer, and woolly rhinoceros. Hunted by man, and gradually deprived of their natural food, they died out, and only their bones remain to tell us that once they roamed our land.

The icy wastes, dotted with tiny willow and birch trees, were slowly transformed by the growing warmth until they became forest lands, the haunts of the red deer, the wild ox, and the pig, which had migrated from warmer lands in the south.

Some of the Old Stone Age (Palaeolithic) people were able to change their way of life, and so survived into the warmer phase of climate. They had to learn the habits of the forest animals and to recognize the new nuts and berries which could be eaten; and the sea-shore and the sea itself began to provide them with foods in the form of fish and shell-fish which had not been able to exist in the extreme cold of the previous age.

About 8,000 years ago Britain began to take shape almost as we now see it on a map. The land began to sink so that its lower parts became covered with the sea. Where these low lands had been forested the trunks of the trees soon disappeared, but the lower parts and the roots remained fixed in the ground and may often still be seen round our coasts. Examples of these 'submerged forests' occur at low tide near Dover in Kent, Hastings and Bexhill in Sussex, Polperro in Cornwall, Porlock and Minehead in Somerset, and Brancaster in Norfolk. There are submerged forests of very much earlier date, as at Lulworth Cove in Dorset, but these are fossilized and not usually found just below the level of low tide.

Round about 6000 B.C. much of what we now know as the North Sea was formed. Before that time its southern half, from Yorkshire to northern Denmark, could be crossed on foot, and we know that people were moving over to Britain, hunting as they went, for one of their fish-spears made of bone was drawn up in a fishing net about twenty-five miles off the Norfolk coast. In the same area stumps of pine trees are sometimes found in the nets.

But there is little that you can see of these Middle Stone Age (Mesolithic) people. One group, that came from France early in the period, settled in sandy tracts, especially those of southern Britain. If you are very lucky you may discover one of their camping places in a high sandy spot, but the only way you are likely to recognize it is by the scatter of tiny, neat flint implements that they used. Quite often these tools are less than an inch long.

Until about 4,500 years ago man could eat only if he hunted animals and collected fruits and roots. The people of the Old Stone Age and of the Middle Stone Age did not sow and reap and make bread. They did not know how to do so, because the wild grasses from which wheat, rye, barley, and oats were developed could be found only in the ancient Bible lands round the eastern Mediterranean. There the art of growing food was discovered about 6,000–7,000 years ago. Everywhere else in Europe, Asia, and Africa people lived, as they did in Britain, by their skill in hunting. But the discovery of agriculture did not make hunting unnecessary, although it did provide a small but fairly certain supply of good body-building food.

The earliest farmers did not know that soil can be manured and so go on producing food almost indefinitely. As their cultivated plots became exhausted of plant-foods their crops became poorer and poorer, and in order to grow enough corn, new land had to be brought into cultivation and the old abandoned. Partly for this reason there began a slow but steady movement of people breaking new soil and gradually moving farther away from the lands of the Bible. But the soils easiest to work do not occur everywhere, and sometimes it must have been necessary to cross wide areas of difficult heavy soil or of poor sandy soil before suitable light soils could be found.

Slowly some of them worked westwards as far as France,

and finally, about 2500 B.C., some of them crossed over to Britain. More than any other people before them these farmers of the New Stone (Neolithic) Age have left widespread signs of their activities in our land, and in later pages we shall see what those signs are. But first let us jump aboard the time machine and take ourselves back to the days when one of the New Stone Age families was preparing to cross over to the South Coast.

The Earliest Farmers

Imagine for a while that we belong to a New Stone Age family that has long been settled on the north coast of France but now finds it necessary to cross over the Channel in search of new land only a few miles across the sea. (The Strait of Dover was very much narrower at that time.)

Drawn up on the beach is a large boat made from a huge oak-trunk which has been hollowed out and shaped by fire. The family dog is running along, wild with excitement, barking as the waves break gently on the shingle. Beneath the cliff a dozen cattle are tethered, frightened, and lowing from time to time because they are thirsty. The herdsman seems to take a long time in giving them water, which he pours from a skin into a roughly-made earthenware bowl. There is room in the boat for only three cattle at a time, but if the sea remains calm all of them can be taken across in the next two days. Then some of the sheep, left in the charge of another old herdsman, can be taken over.

Two great skin bags brim-full of precious wheat and barley grains, seed for corn that must soon be sown, are placed in the stern of the ship. In the bows our mother puts a large bowl and beside it a skin of fresh water, so that the men at the paddles may refresh themselves during the voyage.

As we are watching the boat being made ready, there suddenly comes a loud bellowing, and we turn round to see one of the cattle thrown on its side and its legs tied together with thongs of hide. As even full-grown cattle are small, two men are able to carry each one to the boat, until three of the beasts are placed on their sides amidships, their eyes full of terror. In jumps the dog as the family goes aboard, and soon the men paddling strike up a chant as the heavily laden boat puts out towards the new land.

The sea is calm and there is little wind, but no one dares to move very much, for the boat has no keel and could easily capsize. That is why the cattle had to be bound. In front and to right and left other boats can be seen making in the same direction. This is the first calm day after the harvest has been gathered, and new homes have to be built and new fields broken up from the shrubby waste before the time comes for sowing the corn in the spring.

Towards noon the cliffs, so very like those left behind, seem to get rapidly closer, and course is changed towards a point in the coast where there is a gap in the long uneven crest of the white cliff wall. Run ashore on the crunchy shingle, the boat is drawn up with a great heave out of reach of the waves. Soon the cattle are landed and led to a small clear brook to drink. Then the stores are unloaded and camp is made on a grassy patch above high-tide mark. Even before the skin tents are pitched mother has made a fire and is cooking corn porridge.

After the meal our two eldest brothers push off in the boat to fetch more of the cattle and stores. Meanwhile, with father, we find a way to the top of the cliffs, and for a time watch the boat as it slowly makes its way to the opposite shore.

Once the boat has got beyond hailing distance we turn

our eyes towards the new land which is to be ours. Everywhere on the high rolling downs to which we have climbed we see thorn trees and brambles, which cease only on the lower slopes where the dark and silent beech-woods begin. We shall not be short of wood for our fires, or for the very many other uses to which we can put it. And we are delighted to see on the ground many great nodules of unbroken flint. From it we can make our knives, saws, hoes, and axes, and freshly broken flint gives a much better edge.

We make our way as fast as we can through the thorny undergrowth to a high knoll, which has been kept freer of bushes by the strong winds which blow in high places. As we force our way upward a deer dashes away into the thicket, leaping high at every step to clear the tangled scrub. Then we stop in fear. From near by comes the heavy snort of a wild boar. But instead of making the usual fierce attack, he lumbers away, crashing through the bushes, flattening them as though they were slender grass.

On reaching the hilltop we see a wonderful sight. Stretching away from the foot of the downs into the blue distance is a vast shaggy forest, broken only by the silvery gleam of rivers and lakes and by the smaller marsh-loving trees that fringe their shores. Near the foot of the downs is a broad shallow lagoon and we can see at one end the dam that the beavers have built to hold back the water.

Not far distant is a line of lower hills where the trees grow less thickly. Here and there bright orange patches of sand tell us that it is soil not fit for our herds or our homes. Good grass for grazing could not thrive on it nor could our corn be grown there with success. And then suddenly we notice the blue smoke of camp fires, several of them, spread out along the ridge. The smoke of each stands straight up like a ghostly column in the still clear air and flattens high up into long wisps where it is blown by a gentle breeze. But our alarm is soon stilled. Father reminds us of seeing the same thing in sandy country in our old homeland.

These are the camp fires of the simple people whose flint tools are so small. They live by hunting and do not know how to keep cattle for their milk and flesh, or how to grow corn. They are a harmless people, seldom seen, and always ready to flee in terror from the men of our tribe.

Camps and Burial-mounds

Remounting the time-machine we return to the present to discover what remains from the New Stone Age to remind us of the invasion of Britain by the first farming folk. We should expect, first of all, to find some of their fields. But all of them have been ploughed away by later farmers. There are some people who believe that New Stone Age fields are still to be found on Dartmoor in Devon and on Bodmin Moor in Cornwall. They are quite small plots, from which the stones have been gathered and dumped round the edges, and it is the lines of stones that make it possible to see the plots clearly after so long a time. (See p. 98.) It is most likely, however, that these small fields belonged to farmers of the Bronze Age, and we shall therefore consider them in a later chapter.

Ploughs were not known to the earliest farmers, and the turf was broken up for sowing corn by using hoes. This must have been a back-breaking job, and was probably done by the women, who also had the task of making the earthenware pots which had so many uses. The cleaning of skins for clothes and for many other purposes, the weaving of baskets, and the cooking of meals were also women's tasks. The men looked after the herds and added to the food supply by hunting and trapping wild animals in pits. Both men and women cut the corn and gathered it in. Time was

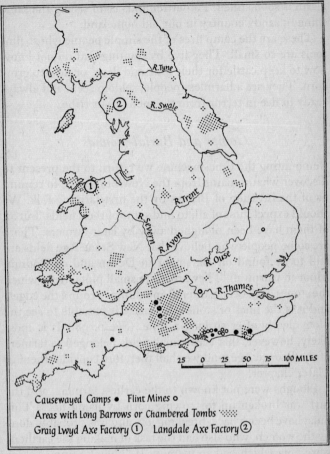

R. Tyne

②

R. Swale

①

R. Trent

R. Severn

R. Avon

R. Ouse

R. Thames

25 0 25 50 75 100 MILES

Causewayed Camps ● Flint Mines ○
Areas with Long Barrows or Chambered Tombs ∷∷∷
Graig Lwyd Axe Factory ① Langdale Axe Factory ②

The regions of New Stone Age Settlement

too short and the crop too valuable for it to be left for the
women to do unaided. The corn was probably cut with
flint sickles, for those which have been found still show on
their edges a golden sheen left by the touch of multitudes of

stalks. But the same sheen would have been left by the cutting of grass for cattle-fodder, so that we cannot be quite sure that the sickles were used in harvesting corn. Probably they were used for both purposes.

On the chalk hills of southern England there are about half a dozen places where we know that people of the New Stone Age lived during the summer months of each year. Many more such places must have existed before modern farmers began ploughing the tops of the downs, not knowing that they were destroying farms four thousand years old. It is still possible to rediscover some of these vanished sites from an aeroplane, and it is quite likely that there are still a few of them faintly visible at some seasons to anyone on the ground.

I called these places 'farms' just now, though they were in fact only enclosures where cattle were kept safe from wolves and bears. Round about them our earliest cornfields must have been carved from the thin soil, and in the ditches families squatted in flimsy and filthy huts. Usually these farms are called 'camps', but they were actually pens for cattle and the summer homes of peaceful peasants; they were not intended for soldiers.

Let us in imagination go for an excursion into the very heart of southern England (see map on p. 58) and visit the most famous of them, Windmill Hill. This site is so famous that from it one large group of New Stone Age people have been named the Windmill Hill Folk, as it was here that their remains were first found and their way of life made known. Round the upper part of the hill we can still trace a section of the low banks arranged roughly in three circles. They are broken here and there by flat spaces, and were originally much higher. On top of them a fence of thorn or of closely set poles was built to keep out wild beasts. The fences gave protection to the cattle, sheep, and pigs, which

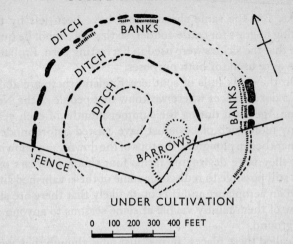

The New Stone Age. Plan of the causewayed camp on
Windmill Hill, Avebury, Wilts

were brought in at night from the vast pastures that lay all
around.

When a part of this camp was carefully excavated it was
found that ditches had been dug down into the chalk and
the spoil from them was piled up just inside the circle, so

New Stone Age flint
axe, Grime's Graves,
Weeting, Norfolk

making the long banks on which the
fences were built. Flint axes were used
to cut down the young trees for the
fences, and some of these axes were
unearthed from beneath the turf in the
camp. Other finds included pieces of
pottery (the oldest kind yet found in
Britain) which look like scraps of a
leather bag. When these people learned
how to make pots to hold water they
copied the shape and appearance of the
leathern vessels which they had always

28

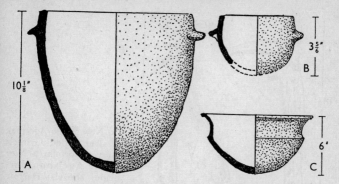

New Stone Age pots from (A) The Trundle, Goodwood, Sussex;
(B) Norton Bavant long barrow, Wilts; and (C) Hanging Grimston
long barrow, Yorks

used for holding water. There can be little doubt that skins
continued to be employed to bring up larger quantities of
water from the brook just below the hill to the east. It would
have needed very many weary journeys up and down hill to
bring enough water in their rather small pots.

Other things that came to light were beautiful little flint
arrow heads about an inch long and shaped like a leaf. These
were used with bows for hunting wild beasts. The stag
especially provided good meat, and his antlers made good
picks and levers for digging into the chalk. For shovels the
shoulder-blades of oxen were used. Broad flat stones, worn
slightly hollow in the middle, were employed for the grinding of corn into flour. The grains
were placed on the top of the stone
and rubbed round with a smaller bun-
shaped stone until flour was produced.
In the flour there was always much
grit caused by the two stones wearing
each other away. When the skulls of
New Stone Age people are found in

New Stone Age arrow-
head of Windmill type,
Essex coast

29

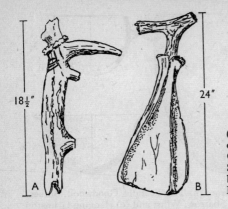

(A) New Stone Age pick of deer antler, Grime's Graves, Norfolk; (B) New Stone Age shoulder-blade shovel, Harrow Hill flint mines, Worthing

their great burial houses their teeth are usually worn flat by the grit that they chewed with their bread.

At several places on the South Downs in Sussex, on Easton Down in Wiltshire, at Peppard in the Chiltern Hills in Oxfordshire, and at a spot wrongly called Grime's Graves near Weeting in west Norfolk, mines have been discovered which were first dug by men of the New Stone Age to obtain the flint which was so important to them in their everyday life (see map on p. 26).

Flint picked up from the surface of the ground is less tough than that which is taken fresh from the chalk; and so much did early man value good flint that he went to the enormous labour of digging shafts down through thirty to forty feet of hard chalk, and from the bottom of a shaft, where good flint was found, he would dig low tunnels in all directions, following seams of the precious stone. He had no pickaxes or shovels of hard-wearing iron. Instead he used parts of antlers from the red deer, trimmed to suit his particular job. With these and a hammer-stone he could lever out lumps of chalk and burrow his way farther and farther from the light of day. One of these antler-picks,

The New Stone Age. Flint mine shaft and galleries,
Harrow Hill, Worthing, Sussex

found in a mining gallery at 'Grime's Graves', still shows the chalky finger-prints of a miner.

As he went downwards making a shaft, and then branched off sideways digging a gallery, the miner had to get rid of great quantities of useless chalk. This he shovelled up with the shoulder-blade of an ox into a wicker basket and carried to the gallery last worked out. When the disused galleries were full, the chalk had to be hauled to the surface and dumped in other old mine-shafts. In the darkness of the galleries chalk or pottery lamps, shaped like a rough shallow cup, were used. These were filled with animal fat, and a moss wick floated on its surface. Here and there in the mines can be seen sooty patches left by the feeble smoky lamps.

The flint that was hauled to the surface was usually trimmed in a workshop set up in a mine-shaft that had almost been filled. The roughly shaped axes were then traded to other tribes far and wide for the cutting down of trees from which to make all the many wooden articles that were so necessary before man discovered the use of metals.

An exciting find in Grime's Graves was a little chalk figure of a goddess resting upon a ledge that looked like an altar. A pile of antler-picks lay at her feet as an offering, for this shaft had disappointed the miners; it did not reach good flint at the usual level. Before filling it up with chalk thrown out from their next shaft they went through a ceremony to persuade the goddess to be kinder to them in their new attempt.

Other little goddesses were found in the camp at Windmill Hill and in the earliest earthwork at Maiden Castle in Dorset, but we know little about the religion of these people. They had some belief in a life after death, for in many parts of Britain they built vast houses of earth or stone for the dead, and these long barrows, as they are called, are the commonest New Stone Age things to be seen.

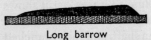

Long barrow

Wherever he made his home and ploughed his fields New Stone Age man heaped up these enormous family tombs (Pl. 1a.). On the chalk downs of Hampshire, Wiltshire, and Dorset, and on the limestone hills of the Cotswolds, they sometimes cluster thickly together. In Kent, Sussex, Lincolnshire, and East Yorkshire more are to be found. In the western mountainous regions, tombs built of great stones replace the earthen long barrows of central and eastern England. These stone-built tombs were erected by peoples of a different origin. The megalithic (big-stone) graves of Cornwall, Wales, and all the rocky highlands round the Irish Sea are of several kinds, but their builders had all arrived by sea from west and south-west Europe. They had slowly spread from the Mediterranean lands into all the mountainous regions that border the Atlantic Ocean in Spain, Portugal, France, and the British Isles. The map on page 26 shows where they are to be found in Britain.

When carefully excavated, long barrows reveal all sorts of local fashions in the way the inner burial chambers were built (Pls. 2a and 2b). From the outside, however, they all look much the same. In southern England, where there was plenty of fine earth to be scraped up from the ground surface, they may be from 75 to 300 feet long and between 45 and 100 feet wide. After many centuries of wearing down they are sometimes still as much as twelve feet high, with the taller and broader end of the mound facing roughly to the eastward. In some of them there was originally a wooden room to hold the dead, but this has long ago rotted away and collapsed, usually leaving little trace but a small dent on the outside of the barrow. Excavation by a treasure-hunter, who did not restore the mound as he found it, leaves a similar hollow in it.

If you look carefully when the sun is low in the morning or evening and casting long shadows, you may see the faint hollow of a ditch running along each side of the barrow, but not round either end. From these two ditches some of the earth and chalk was quarried to make the mound.

In western districts, where stone is easily obtained, a chamber was often built of great blocks, two or more upright and one or more across the top, from which led a passage. On each side of the passage were little rooms to hold the dead bodies. The arrangement of these small chambers is seldom the same in any two long barrows: but if you go to Stoney Littleton in Somerset or to Hetty Pegler's Tump near Uley in Gloucestershire, you may go right inside the barrows and see for yourself what they are like. At Uley

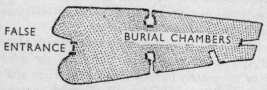

FALSE ENTRANCE   BURIAL CHAMBERS

The New Stone Age. Plan of Belas Knap long barrow near Winchcomb, Glos.

the entrance lies between two projecting horns, and at first there appears to be a similar entrance at Belas Knap just south of Winchcomb, but it is actually a dummy and leads nowhere. There is solid earth behind it. You will notice the dry-stone walling (that is, stones put together without mortar, like many of the field-divisions of the Cotswolds and other stone regions). This occurs all round the barrow at its foot. On the north-east side is the entrance to one of the burial chambers.

The horns enclose a space which was used for ceremonies at the time of burying the dead. Fires were lit and animals were slaughtered and sacrificed; and after liquids had been poured out ceremoniously in honour of the gods, the pottery vessels were smashed deliberately so that they should not be used again. The trampled earth suggests that there was wild dancing as well. Traces of all these customs have been discovered on the old soil-surface in front of the entrances of some of the long barrows.

Some of the dead were kept for a long time before burial. The flesh had rotted from the corpse and the bones fallen apart. Not long ago an undisturbed chamber was found in the Lanhill long barrow near Chippenham, Wiltshire. Seven skeletons of people varying in age from 12 to over 50 lay inside. Their skulls showed that they had all belonged to one family group. Usually tomb-robbers have emptied the burial chambers long ago, but sometimes when an undisturbed barrow has been opened it is obvious that when a new body was put into the tomb the older skeletons were just pushed into a heap on one side.

In some regions, round mounds cover burials of the New Stone Age; in others, such as Yorkshire, the dead were partly or completely burned after burial. Here and there, especially in Wales and Cornwall, the earth or stones that covered a barrow have been carted away, and the chamber that was once buried beneath now stands alone as two or three great upright stones with a large cap-stone across the top of them. (Pls. 2a and 2b). On maps and in guide books these are often called *dolmens* or *cromlechs*. It used not to be realized that these great stone structures (megaliths) are the remains of burial mounds. It is useful to know also that modern maps mark barrows as *tumuli* (the Latin word for 'hillocks'): a single barrow is referred to as a *tumulus*. In the North a barrow is often called a 'law' or 'low', but these words are also applied to natural hills. In various parts of England the words burgh, butt, hill, howe, toot, cop, or tump may be used in the local name of a barrow.

Besides the Windmill Hill people, who were farmers, and who buried their dead in long barrows, the older Middle Stone Age tribes lived on and learned much from the new-comers. Most of the older tribes lived in the eastern half of Britain on the lower ground along the rivers and near the coast. They were joined by people from across the North Sea, who had also learned new ways from tribes that had moved slowly from farther east. In Britain we call these people of the lowlands the Peterborough Folk, because an important discovery of their remains was made on a ridge overlooking the Fens near Peterborough.

They kept to the Middle Stone Age customs of hunting and fishing, but they also learned to tame and breed cattle, and their curved flint sickles suggest that they grew corn. Their pots were made as far as possible to look like wicker-work just as the Windmill Hill people at first made theirs as copies of leathern vessels. As hunters they used bows and arrows, but instead of the neat leaf-shaped flint tips of the Windmill Hill people, they used strange lop-sided ones that you would not expect to fly straight through the air.

These two peoples of the New Stone Age could live in the same land without quarrelling because those to the west

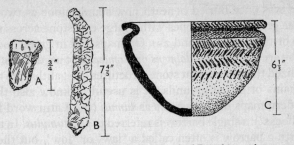

The New Stone Age: (A) Arrowhead of Peterborough type,
Essex coast; (B) Flint sickle, Grovehurst, Kent; (C) Peterborough type pot, the Thames, Mortlake

preferred hill-country and those to the east lived and hunted
in the valleys. But the two people did mix. Sherds (broken
pieces) of Peterborough pots came to light even at Windmill
Hill itself; and sometimes Peterborough ware has turned up
in the long barrows. The lowland people gradually spread
westward and made themselves very useful to the downland
tribes. The hunters became miners and delved in flint
workings in Wiltshire, Sussex, and Norfolk, and their hunting probably enabled them to supply the antlers so necessary in the mines. On their expeditions in search of game
they carried with them goods which Windmill Hill farmers
could not get for themselves, since they had to stay at home
to look after their fields and cattle. As traders the Peterborough people carried stone axes from factories set up on
open mountainsides in North Wales and Cumberland, and
from the flint mines (see map on p. 26). With the axes the
farmers could cut down the woods and break up more
downland turf to form further fields to grow corn. The
Peterborough traders, no longer able to produce food for
themselves since they were always on the move, obtained
corn for bread-making from the stay-at-home farmers in
exchange for the stone and flint axes.

Except for their pottery and tools, which can be seen in some museums, there is nothing visible left of the Peterborough Folk. Very little remains to be seen of the few hut sites and burials that have been discovered in recent years, and you are likely to search in vain for their traces in the open air.

Another people descended from Middle Stone Age tribes is known to have lived in two villages in the Orkney Islands, the one at Skara Brae on the west coast of Mainland, the other at Rinyo on Rousay Island. Skara Brae had for long been covered with wind-blown sand, and was so well preserved that even the stone furniture within the houses had remained undisturbed. A few potsherds like some from Skara Brae have turned up in Wiltshire and on the Essex coast, but their presence has not yet been properly explained. Some of it was found in the great encircling ditch at Stonehenge, with flint flakes and other objects belonging to the end of the New Stone Age and the beginning of the Early Bronze Age. Other scraps were discovered at Woodhenge near Stonehenge and in various parts of southern and eastern England. From its appearance this kind of pottery is called grooved ware.

The New Stone Age. Sherds of grooved ware, Woodhenge, Durrington, Wilts

It is likely that the Orkney villages continued to be lived in by the same people for long after the Windmill Hill tribes had been conquered by men using flint or bronze daggers and beaker-shaped pots. The Peterborough traders, following their old hunting trails with a stock of axes, were still very useful, and when their farmer-customers had been overcome by new war-lords, they probably changed their stocks to suit the new customers and hawked around the countryside the ores of copper and tin out of which weapons of bronze were made. These ores had to be carried from the west of Britain like some of the stone axes, and gradually definite trade routes came to be established. The traders seem to have become quite important, for some of them were buried in the long barrows and others in the earth and timber temples about which we shall soon be hearing.

It is important to remember that the Peterborough Folk did not just disappear when men of the Bronze Age invaded Britain, but that they found new ways of being useful and of earning the food which they did not grow for themselves. Mixed with other tribes they became in time the most important people in Britain, and the Food Vessel people and the Urn Folk of the Middle and Late Bronze Ages were in part their descendants.

Between 1900 and 1800 B.C. there was a slight sinking of the land, and on the east coast, at any rate, the sea invaded it, leaving a layer of buttery clay. Just beneath this layer scraps of Windmill Hill, Peterborough, and grooved ware pots have been recovered at different places; and on the same level were sherds of beaker, the earliest kind of Bronze Age pottery. This indicates when the land sank, and that the tribes using these various kinds of pottery were living at about the same time.

In the same period the climate began to change. For about 3,500 years the weather had been moist and warm; now it slowly turned drier, though the warmth of summer continued much as before. But the drier climate resulted in changes in the commoner plants. For long the pine and the hazel had been the most common trees; now the swamp-loving alder, the oak, elm, and lime gradually spread north-ward and increased in numbers. These facts are important to remember because, although few wooden objects survive from these early times, there must have been many of them in every household. The oak and the lime are both especially useful woods to primitive people.

Things to be seen in the Open Air

CAUSEWAYED CAMPS. Two of the easiest to understand when you walk over them are Windmill Hill, near Avebury (and don't forget the Avebury Museum), and Knap Hill, seven miles south-west of Marlborough. Slight remains of others may be seen at Robin Hood Ball, two and a half miles north-east of Shrewton, Wilts; at Hembury, five miles north-west of Honiton in east Devon; at the Trundle, Goodwood, Sussex; at White-hawk, near Brighton; Combe Hill, near Eastbourne; and half ploughed out on Barkhale Down, Bignor, Sussex. At Hembury and the Trundle the obvious earthworks are of the Early Iron Age; you have to search for traces of the causewayed camp. A new one has recently been found in western Wiltshire. The one at Maiden Castle is completely covered by the later ramparts. Don't expect too much from these camps, for there is little to see; but they are the oldest surviving British earthworks.

FLINT MINES. These look like a lot of bumps and hollows, quite unlike the usual smooth turf of the chalk downs. They may be seen at Harrow Hill about six miles north-west of Worthing, Sussex, and within the Iron Age hill-fort of Cissbury, four miles north of Worthing. Others may be found on Bow Hill, Stoke Down, Church Hill (Findon) and on Lavant Down, all a few miles north or north-west of Chichester, and on Wind-over Hill, four miles north-west of Eastbourne, where there is also a long barrow. The most interesting mines are those wrongly called Grime's Graves, five miles north-west of Thetford in east Norfolk. There you are allowed to descend two shafts and inspect the galleries. Those on Easton Down, Wiltshire, are inaccessible. (All are shown on the map on p. 26.)

FIELDS. On Dartmoor, Exmoor, and Bodmin Moor, but since they are probably of later date, they will be mentioned under the Bronze Age.

LONG BARROWS AND MEGALITHS (Big-stone monuments). There are so very many of these that I can mention only a few besides those talked about in this chapter. Salisbury Plain has many, but perhaps the finest is Tilshead Old Ditch, eleven miles south of Devizes. It is 390 feet long, and near it are several more long barrows. There are many more in the Cotswolds than those already described, and others still to be discovered. On the downs of Sussex, Hampshire, and Dorset, close to the North Downs of Kent, on the Lincolnshire Wolds, and on the limestone hills of North Yorkshire between Scarborough and Pickering many are known and probably there are a few more still to be found. In the more mountainous districts a few occur near the Peak of Derbyshire (stone burial chambers in *round* not long barrows), and in Cornwall, north-west Wales, Anglesey, and in Pembrokeshire. In mountain regions the burials are usually made in cairns, that is, piles of stones. (See map, p. 26.)

In Museums

Polished stone axes, querns for grinding corn, pottery, flint sickles, arrow heads, and skeletons from tombs. The following exhibit small or large collections of New Stone Age objects: British Museum, London; National Museum of Wales, Cardiff; University Museums at Oxford and Cambridge; Avebury, Devizes, and Salisbury, Wiltshire; Lewes and Worthing, Sussex; Dorchester and Farnham, Dorset; Thetford and Norwich, Norfolk; York, Hull, and Bridlington, Yorkshire; Peterborough, Northamptonshire; Newcastle, Northumberland. The Ipswich Museum has many objects from Grime's Graves. Almost every town with a museum has a little to show of this period.

2: The Coming of Bronze

THE BRONZE AGE began in Britain between 1,900 and 1,800 years before the birth of Christ and lasted for about 1,400 years. That is just about the same length of time that has passed since Hengist and Horsa landed in Kent with the first war-bands of English. There was no sudden widespread use of bronze exactly as the year 1850 B.C. was reached. The first users of it were invaders, and only about one in twenty of them could afford it. There was probably no one in Britain at this time who knew how to dig for copper and tin ores, smelt away the impurities, and then cast the molten metal into weapons; that knowledge came from Ireland later. In Britain hundreds of years passed before bronze implements became common or before skill in bronze-smithing was widespread.

Instead of bronze, flint continued in use for the making of most tools, and the miners were kept busy digging up the raw material. Equally busy were the descendants of the Peterborough Folk hawking their wares along the trade routes (see map on p. 85). In fact, flint went on being used for many purposes until centuries even after the coming of iron.

The first invaders of the Bronze Age are called the Beaker Folk, from the shape of the pots they used, and which they buried with their dead (see B and D overleaf). Hundreds of years earlier they had begun moving westwards from the lands round the eastern Mediterranean and had settled in Spain, where their beaker pots have been found with burials. From Spain they spread into France and into

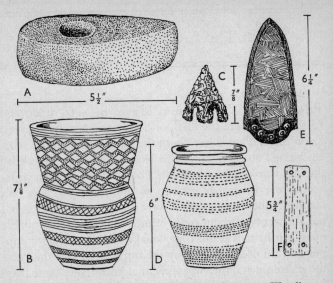

The Beaker Folk: (A) Axe of Cornish granite, from near Woodhenge; (B) 'A', or later type beaker, Wilts; (C) Flint arrow-head, Essex coast; (D) 'B', or earlier type beaker, Suffolk; (E) Bronze dagger, Homington, Wilts; (F) Bone wrist-guard, Roundway Down, Wilts

Western Germany and Holland, mixing with the older peoples of those regions and especially with the tribes whose main weapon was the stone battle-axe (see A above). From Germany and Holland groups crossed over to southern and eastern Britain in scattered bands, landing in Sussex and along the East Coast from Kent to Yorkshire as well as in mid-Scotland. Other groups came over a little later from Brittany (western France) to Dorset (see B above). The Beaker people did not all arrive at the same time, and the later bands were larger than the earlier. Among the later invaders came some of the Battle-Axe Folk with whom the Beaker people had mixed in Holland and Germany.

We know little about the houses that these people built,

although pieces of their pots have been found in roughly circular shallow pits, which were very probably the floors of their huts. The walls may have been of wickerwork daubed with clay to keep out the weather, and wickerwork covered with skins is likely to have formed the roof. On Easton Down, Wiltshire, close to the shafts of the flint mines, the hut floors were of many irregular shapes but seldom more than six feet across or more than eighteen inches deep. Surrounding the outside of the hut floors on Easton Down the excavators found holes six inches wide and six inches deep, which once had held pointed stakes to support the hut walls. In addition to pieces of beaker pottery, pot-boilers, flint tools, and bones of ox, pig, and sheep were found. These tell us something about their food and their way of life.

Pot-boilers, which can sometimes be picked up where ancient man had his dwelling, are stones, usually rounded ones, that have been cracked and split by heating. Some kinds of pottery will break if put over a fire. But water had to be heated to cook food, and this was done by putting stones in the fire, and when they had become red hot, dropping them into the cooking-pot. The first few stones would be cracked when dropped into a cold liquid for the same reason that a cold glass tumbler will crack if you pour hot milk into it.

Cooking must have been done in the open, where many more of the pot-boilers and quantities of ash from fires were found. Several huts seem to have shared one cooking-place. On the edge of Mildenhall Fen, Cambridgeshire, the relics of a cannibal feast were found among household rubbish. Samples of wood and bone ash from Easton Down were sent to Vienna for study under the microscope. Some very tiny particles of charcoal occurred in the ash, and it was possible for a scientist to say that some of the charcoal was produced by burning wood from coniferous trees (like fir and pine) and that the rest of it came from deciduous trees (such as oak, ash, or hazel). This gives us some idea of the woods that existed not far from Easton Down nearly 3,800 years ago. Deciduous and coniferous woodlands are still to be found over a large area just to the south.

The commonest things of the Beaker Folk remaining to-day are their burials, which are quite frequently discovered. Usually the body was buried with the knees drawn up to the chin, which is the position in which primitive people are said to sleep. And it looks as if the Beaker Folk thought that their dead had in fact gone to sleep, and would wake up in a new life in which they would need many of the things that they had owned before falling asleep.

Behind the feet of the skeleton, or elsewhere in the grave, was placed a beaker containing drink (see p. 42, figures B and D); and near the waist the excavator finds a flint, copper, or bronze dagger (see p. 42, figure E), originally held in place by a belt and scabbard; but the leather has long ago rotted away to nothing. Often beside the wrist of the skeleton is a thin, oblong piece of stone or bone slightly hollow on one side and with tiny holes in the corners (see p. 42, figure F). This is a wrist-guard to protect the archer when he released an arrow; for the bow-string flies back with a stinging blow immediately the arrow takes flight. To complete the archer's equipment a bow and usually one arrow were put in the grave, but the wooden parts have gone, and only a beautifully chipped arrow-head of flint remains (figure C).

Above the body of a Beaker man his tribesmen piled up a circular mound of earth, each one bringing a wicker basketful to tip on the growing mound. Sometimes the barrow was begun by the digging of a ring-ditch round the corpse and throwing the soil over it. Other barrows were finished by the digging of the ditch, and on the downs the chalk dug from the ditch was put on last. Frost and rain soon turned this loose chalk into a grey-white crust all over the barrow. As it was usually built on high ground the white barrow must have shown up clearly for miles.

Some Early and Middle Bronze Age barrows have no ditch and are called bowl barrows; others have a space, called a berm, left between the foot of the mound and the inner edge of the ditch so that the earth would not slip down the mound straight into it and fill it up. Those with a berm and a ditch are called bell barrows. There are several other forms

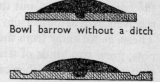

Bowl barrow without a ditch

Bell barrow

of tumuli, especially later in the Bronze Age, but bowl and bell barrows are by far the commonest kinds (Pl. 3a).

Beaker warriors may be buried singly in flat graves, or in cemeteries of up to twenty burials. In districts where stone was plentiful, as on Dartmoor, the body was laid in a box, called a cist, made of slabs of stone (Pl. 3b). In the same kind of district the mound is often a heap of stones and is called a cairn.

Two warriors' graves contained the heads of the hawks with which they hunted smaller birds for food. In a few graves gold ornaments, such as ear-rings, have been found. In other burials slight traces of a fine cloth, woven from the fibres of stinging-nettles, have been detected.

The Beaker warriors may have been rather like the Normans, in that they came over to Britain in fighting bands and became the overlords of the people they conquered. Occasionally they mixed with the New Stone Age tribes and were buried in the long barrows. Scraps of their beaker-pots have sometimes been found in them. The Beaker people had broad round skulls, but the New Stone Age farmers had long narrow skulls, so that it is easy to pick out the burial of a Beaker man or woman from the other skeletons in a long barrow.

From the little we know about the ordinary life of the overlords it seems that they preferred to keep herds of cattle, pigs, and sheep rather than to hoe the soil and grow corn. It is true that the impress of grains of barley has been found on the bases of beakers, but this corn could easily have been received as a tribute from the New Stone Age farmers. These, as we know from the impressions of grains on their pots, grew two kinds of wheat, the one called short-eared club wheat and the other called small spelt. (These are, of course, the modern names; nothing is known of the languages spoken before the later Bronze Age.) If the Beaker people could demand corn from their subjects, they would not trouble to learn how to grow it for themselves.

No doubt these warriors delighted to use their skill with the bow in hunting wild animals. Probably a favourite quarry was the *Urus*, a gigantic ox that stood six feet high at the shoulder, and was prized, perhaps, for its large shoulder-blades, which were so useful as shovels in the flint mines. This great beast survived in Poland until the eighteenth century. Other beasts of the chase were the wolf and the bear, which continue to live in some parts of Europe even at the present day, though in Britain they have been extinct for hundreds of years. Deer and boar were hunted too, because they provided meat in winter when the cattle were skinny through lack of fodder. In any case it was necessary to kill off all but a few breeding cattle in the autumn because there was little to feed them on until the new growth of grass in the following spring. The introduction of the turnip as a fodder crop about two hundred years ago made it possible to feed cattle right through the winter and so provide supplies of fresh meat throughout the year.

Things to be seen in the Open Air

ROUND BARROWS, in large numbers on Salisbury Plain and the southern chalk downs. In smaller numbers they can be seen in most regions where prehistoric man lived.

HENGE MONUMENTS – see pp. 65-6.

In Museums

Beakers, flint, copper and bronze daggers, flint arrow-heads and wrist-guards. In a few museums a complete Beaker burial with skeleton and grave-goods is shown. Many of the museums listed at the end of the last chapter exhibit Early Bronze Age objects, but there are also many small local museums with something to show of this period.

The Earliest Heathen Temples

Although the detective of ancient things (properly called an archaeologist) does much of his work on or just beneath the surface of the ground, he nowadays also uses an aeroplane whenever he can in order to get a bird's-eye view of the works of prehistoric man. From the air the whole plan of the works becomes clearer. A muddle of faint ditches and banks, as seen from ground level, takes on a pattern with a meaning when seen from above; and many new pieces, invisible from the ground, are added to the pattern when looked at from the air. Indeed, even when nothing at all has been visible for many centuries, an aerial view will rediscover temples, houses, villages, barrows, hill-forts, defensive ditches, roads, and tracks. Once the earth has been cut into, the disturbance always leaves some traces. From the ground these can be understood only at a distance and at one season of the year, or in the morning or evening light when the sun is low, or even after a long drought or during a shallow flood; but one day they are noticed from an aeroplane, and a camera comes into action to make a lasting record of them. Some time later, excavation may start with the exact position of all parts of the site clearly known from the air-photograph. That is how we have come to know as much as we do about ancient temples during the last thirty years.

Altogether about forty of these temples have now been discovered in Britain, and new examples are found almost every year, sometimes in large groups. Aerial photographs of fields between Abingdon and Wallingford, near the Thames south of Oxford, show that this was a sacred region in very early times. Several kinds of earthworks and barrows were seen which the plough had flattened hundreds of years ago, but they were easily visible as marks in the crops.

Three separate groups showed up near the villages of Sutton Courtenay, Benson, and Dorchester. The last of these groups of earthworks, and the one that looks the most interesting, was in danger of being destroyed by gravel-digging, and it was decided to investigate their date and purpose before they disappeared for ever (Pl. 1b).

One of the results of the Dorchester excavations is that we can now distinguish more clearly between two main kinds of temple. The first kind has only one entrance and the second usually has two. Both kinds often have a circular ditch all round, and the earth from it is almost always heaped in the form of a circular bank just outside the ditch. The fact that it is outside shows that these earthworks were not meant as a protection like the banks and ditches of a hill-fort.

The first kind, then, has one entrance through the surrounding circular bank and ditch. Within the circle excavation brings to light a series of pits, often arranged in a smaller circle, and in some of the pits pottery of the Peterborough Folk and of the Grooved-Ware people has been found (see drawings on pp. 36 and 37).

At Stonehenge you can see an outer bank and ditch, the one worn down and the other nearly filled up. These are all that remain visible of the earliest temple; the great stone circles and horseshoes were put up at a later time. In the lowest part of the ditch, which, as always, began slowly filling up as soon as it was dug, scraps of grooved ware pots were found with flint flakes and tools like those found in the flint mines on Easton Down, nine miles to the south-east. The mines were begun by the Peterborough tribes. There were other objects in the Stonehenge ditch belonging to the end of the New Stone Age or to the very beginning of the Early Bronze Age. Further up in the ditch, and so later in the time when they were dropped, were pieces of beaker pot which certainly belong to the Early Bronze Age (see p. 42, figures B and D).

A little more than thirty feet inside the Stonehenge ditch, and only just inside the bank, there was a circle of over fifty round holes, now marked in white chalk. These are called the Aubrey Holes after the man who discovered them in the seventeenth century. A number of them have been opened at different times, and some archaeologists have thought that the holes once held the great wooden uprights of a vast temple, and others that they were the sockets for great stones. Both of these ideas are wrong. Two new holes were opened in 1950, and one of them contained burnt human bones. The same had been found in other Aubrey Holes excavated some years ago.

It now seems certain that it was a custom at the end of the New Stone Age to burn the corpse and collect the pieces of burnt bone into a skin bag, which was then fastened by

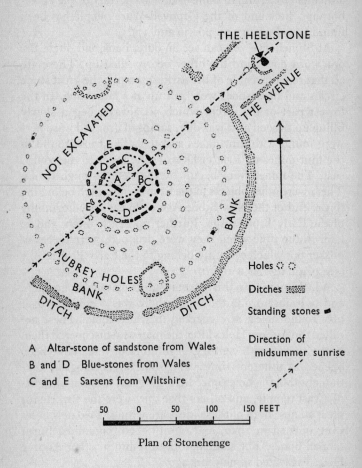

THE HEELSTONE

THE AVENUE

NOT EXCAVATED

THE AVENUE

BANK

AUBREY HOLES

BANK

DITCH

DITCH

Holes

Ditches

Standing stones

Direction of
midsummer sunrise

A   Altar-stone of sandstone from Wales
B and D   Blue-stones from Wales
C and E   Sarsens from Wiltshire

50   0   50   100   150 FEET

Plan of Stonehenge

means of a long bone pin. The bag was then buried in a hole. It was not a custom of the Windmill Hill farmers, who in fact did not burn their dead, though some of the great stone tombs of northern Ireland were used for cremation burials of this kind. But it is likely that the builders of the great stone tombs belonged to tribes different from the Windmill Hill people. At Stonehenge it must have been the Peterborough or the Grooved-Ware Folk who used the place as a cremation cemetery and the ditch and the Aubrey Holes for burnt burials. Four of the long bone pins were found with the ashes of the dead, but the skin bags that had held the ashes had rotted away long ago and completely disappeared. Similar burnt burials with pins were found at Dorchester and at Duggleby in the East Riding of Yorkshire, and the custom survived into the Middle Bronze Age in Wiltshire, Yorkshire, and other areas.

Five temple sites like the first Stonehenge were discovered at Dorchester, though they were much smaller and could not be seen from ground level until they were excavated. They showed that the Windmill people had some hand in the work but that the Peterborough and Grooved-Ware tribes had a far larger share in them. The Peterborough people were descended, as we have seen, from Middle Stone Age tribes, and they survived, with further changes in their way of life, as the Food Vessel people, who are described in Chapter 3.

Before we leave the subject of the earliest Stonehenge one other very interesting matter ought to be mentioned; it is one of the many marvels of modern science. In one of the Aubrey Holes there were some big lumps of oak charcoal with the burnt bones, the remnants of the funeral pyre on which the body had been destroyed. Some of the charcoal was sent to America, where its radio-active state was studied. It had been active for about 3,800 years, that is, since about 1843 B.C. Although these figures may be too early or too late by as much as 275 years, you can see that they do agree with the date that is usually given for the end of the New Stone Age and the coming of the Beaker tribes in about 1850 B.C. In this method of dating, by measuring the radio-active state of animal or vegetable substances, we have a new and valuable means of roughly checking dates arrived at by very indirect means. The important thing to remember about the Aubrey Holes, however, is that they never held wooden posts or standing stones, though it is possible that a circle of wooden uprights was set up towards the centre of Stonehenge at the time when the outer ditch and Aubrey Holes were dug.

Less than two miles north-east of Stonehenge is the site of a temple called Woodhenge which did have wooden uprights once, and which was discovered from the air. When it was excavated a ditch seven feet deep and fourteen feet wide at the bottom was uncovered. The earth and chalk from it had been thrown outside to form a circular bank which, like the ditch, was not constructed on the north-east side but was broken by an undug causeway, leaving a single entrance. The whole of the temple is about 300 feet across.

Towards the middle were holes in the chalk which had held timber posts, and traces of the wood were actually discovered. The holes were arranged in six circles, one within the other; and those in the third circle from the ditch were the largest, and once contained quite thick tree trunks. Within the innermost circle, near the centre of the temple, the excavators found the skeleton of a baby with its skull split open. The builders of the temple had sacrificed the child when the place was dedicated. A line drawn through this grave along the axis of the monument points north-eastward to the spot on the horizon where the sun is first seen on midsummer's day. The same is true of the first and of the later Stonehenge (see plan, p. 50). The timber up-rights of Woodhenge are now marked by concrete stumps, and they help to make clear its arrangement.

Another monument of wood was found at Arminghall near Norwich by observation from the air. This was somewhat similar to Woodhenge except that it had two ditches with a bank between; and towards the centre there had been a horseshoe arrangement of posts rather like the one of stone in the present Stonehenge. Pottery from the Wiltshire and Norfolk Woodhenges showed that among the builders of both were Beaker people, and particularly those who had crossed over from Holland and north Germany, where there were great forests from which wood could be taken for such monuments. No stone for a temple like Stonehenge is to be found in those countries.

Another of the Dorchester temples had two ditches and two opposite entrances, and between the ditches was a bank as at Arminghall, but no post-holes or burials were dis-covered in it. Pieces of early beaker pottery were, however, found in the lowest part of the inner ditch, and these give its date (about 1800 B.C.). A different kind of earthwork was recently excavated at Dorchester-on-Thames. This whole area, like the Avebury and Stonehenge regions, is closely sprinkled with barrows, although most of those in the Thames valley have long ago been ploughed down. All three regions, and others in Britain, had something especially sacred about them, and to them peoples came to worship and to bury their dead through many ages. We can hardly guess at their religious ceremonies, though clearly the sun was sacred to these ancient peoples for its life-giving power. At any rate, at Dorchester (Dorset) yet another kind of monument, called a *cursus*, came to light (as on map, page 56, and see Pl. 16).

It consisted of two parallel ditches, running from north-west to south-east. A space of about 200 feet is left undisturbed between the ditches, which once extended further at both ends, so that the total length of this cursus was at least three-quarters of a mile. The ditches are V-shaped, and from five to twelve feet wide at the top, and from three and a half to seven feet deep. The earth and gravel from them was thrown up to ground level on the inside of the ditches, forming two long parallel banks with the ditches just outside them. In the ditches the excavators found a leaf-shaped arrow-head and some pieces of New Stone Age pottery as used by the Peterborough Folk (see page 36, figure c). These relics help to prove that the cursus is of almost equal age with some of the temples.

Near Stonehenge there used to be the most famous cursus of all. It was well known to the earlier archaeologists, one of whom was able to draw it, in 1740. Now it is almost all ploughed away except near its western end, three-quarters of a mile north-west of Stonehenge. In many ways it is like the Dorchester cursus. It runs from east to west for nearly two miles, and it is about 330 feet wide. It goes westward from a long barrow downhill and then uphill so that it was possible to see the whole length from any point along it.

Not long ago the western end was carefully excavated. The ditch was found to have a section left undug, like a causeway in a New Stone Age camp. To make the ditch the chalk was loosened with antler picks, and, when a good seam of flint was found by chance, the workmen set about making use of it. Chips from flint tools made on the spot showed that the ditch in two places had become a workshop for shaping axes. But the most exciting discovery of all was a little chip of bluestone that does not naturally occur anywhere in eastern or central England. Some of the stones of Stonehenge are of the same rock. When a very thin slice of the bluestone was studied under a microscope it proved to be of a kind that is found only in the mountains round Milford Haven in the far west of Wales. Further search of a newly ploughed field between Stonehenge and the cursus produced many more flakes of the bluestone, especially close to the cursus.

It is now believed likely that this end of the cursus once contained a circle of bluestones, and that they were taken down, trimmed (hence the flakes lying about), and put up again where we now see them as part of the great Stonehenge monument. A careful inspection of the bluestones shows that one of them had been used earlier as a lintel, lying across the top of two uprights; and it may be that this occurred when all of them were used for an older henge at the western end of the cursus. It is possible to prove that the bluestones arrived from Wales at a time when New Stone Age folk were still burying their dead; for a block of this stone was found inside the covering of earth of a long barrow near Heytesbury, Wiltshire. It was almost certainly gathered with the scrapings of earth when the barrow was being made.

In Dorset, about fifteen miles south-west of Salisbury, yet another cursus can be seen (see map overleaf). It runs south-westwards from near Pentridge for three and a half miles to Gussage Hill, where its ditches point straight to the two ends of a long barrow. On Bottlebush Down, between the Roman road called the Ackling Dyke and the modern road that runs from Handley to Cranborne village, the banks of this cursus may be seen quite clearly. If you look carefully you can see that the Roman road was built later, because it goes over the cursus; and at the Gussage end the banks and ditches of a Romano-British village have destroyed the lines of the cursus, which must therefore have been made earlier than the village. All of these sites are marked on the map overleaf.

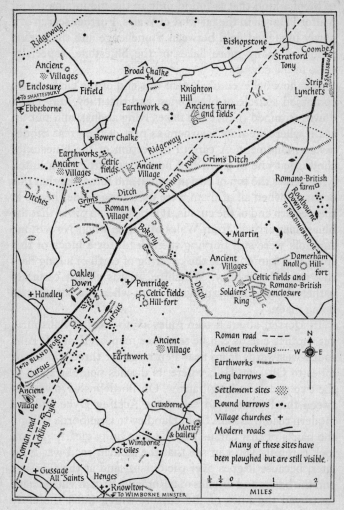

Ridgeway

Bishopstone

Stratford Tony

Coombe

To SALISBURY

Ancient Villages

Broad Chalke

Enclosure

To SHAFTESBURY

Fifield

Knighton Hill

Strip Lynchets

Ebbesborne

Earthwork

Ancient farm and fields

Bower Chalke

Ridgeway

Earthworks Ancient Villages

Celtic fields

Ancient Village

Grim's Ditch

Romano-British farm

Rockbourne Down

To FORDINGBRIDGE

Ditches

Grims

Ditch

Roman road

Roman Village

Bokerly

Martin

Ancient Villages

Damerham Knoll

Hill-fort

Celtic fields and Romano-British enclosure

Soldiers' Ring

Oakley Down

Pentridge

Celtic fields Hill-fort

Ditch

Handley

Cursus

Ancient Village

Earthwork

Cursus

Ancient Village

Cranborne

Roman road Ackling Dyke

Motte & bailey

Wimborne St Giles

Gussage All Saints

Henges

Knowlton

To WIMBORNE MINSTER

Roman road — — —
Ancient trackways ......
Earthworks
Long barrows
Settlement sites
Round barrows ..·.
Village churches +
Modern roads

N
W E
S

Many of these sites have been ploughed but are still visible.

½ ¼ 0   1   2
MILES

Ancient Sites in Cranborne Chase

On Dartmoor there are several double lines of stones with a stone circle at one end and a cairn at the other. The earth covering of the Moor is usually too thin to be sufficient in quantity to allow the making of banks and barrows, and the underlying rock is too hard to be dug, like chalk, with antler-picks. But the arrangement of these stone rows is very like that of the earthen cursus of Wessex. One of the best of the Dartmoor monuments runs south from Green Hill to Stall Moor. There is a cairn at the northern end (like the long barrow of the Stonehenge cursus), and a stone circle at the southern end. You will remember that it is likely that the bluestones once formed a circle at the western end of the Stonehenge cursus. The Dartmoor monument is situated six miles north of Ivybridge, and can be reached along a moorland track from the hamlet of Harford (Ordnance Survey Sheet 187 or 188).

We can only guess the purpose of these sacred sites. Perhaps on certain days in the year people met at one end of the cursus and then went in solemn procession along the avenue between banks or lines of stones to the tomb of a great chief at the other end. Whatever the ceremonies they may have been used for, they are certainly impressive where they survive almost complete as on Dartmoor; and they tell us what hard work ancient peoples would do for the sake of their religion.

Avebury and Stonehenge

Now we turn to the most wonderful of all ancient British temples, Avebury, in northern Wiltshire. Like Stonehenge, this monument was not originally constructed in the form we now see; it has been greatly altered, first in ancient times to a new plan and then in the eighteenth century, when much of it was ignorantly destroyed by local farmers.

The earliest form of the Avebury temple had three great circles of stones in a line, with an avenue of standing stones leading from them. When it was altered in Early Bronze Age times an enormous ditch (Pl. 4a) up to thirty feet wide and thirty feet deep was dug, and the upcast from it was piled on the outside, forming a huge bank. From the top of the bank to the bottom of the ditch is a distance of about fifty feet, and the bank encloses an area of over twenty-eight acres. Just within the ditch the builders placed a hundred stones, of which a few remain (Pl. 4b), spaced twenty-seven feet apart. Within this circle they placed two smaller double circles, and near the centre of the northern inner circle they put three great upright stones, of which only two now remain. The southern inner circle had one great standing stone at its centre. Wherever the old rough-hewn stones once stood there are now small concrete posts that make it possible to understand the original plan.

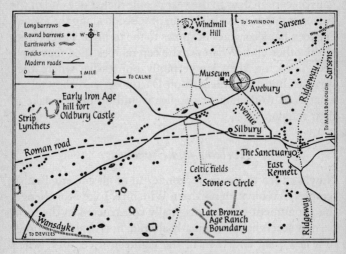

The Avebury district; earthworks of all ages

From the northern circle runs an avenue of stones for a mile and a half to the 'Sanctuary' on Overton Hill. There, where the ancient Ridgeway crosses the present main road, you can see modern stones marking the positions of yet other ancient circles, one within the other (map, opposite). Before the original stones were brought here, there had been a timber monument of six circles, like Woodhenge, except that the Sanctuary never had an outer ditch and bank. Close to one of the stones of the inner ring excavators found the crouched skeleton of a 14-year-old boy, by whose knees lay the broken sherds of a beaker pot. He was of the same long-headed type as are usually found in long barrows, though he was buried in the fashion of a Beaker warrior.

At the foot of several stones in the Avenue leading to the Sanctuary four burials came to light, and with two of them were beakers. Underneath the bank at Avebury, and resting on the original ground surface, pieces of Peterborough pottery were found. This suggests that the whole complex monument was made while the Beaker Folk were overlords, but the boy's skull and the Peterborough sherds suggest that the older tribes may have had a hand in this, or perhaps in the early Avebury temple.

But the greatest mystery of all is Silbury Hill, just a mile to the south of Avebury. This is an enormous barrow 130 feet high, and said to be the largest made by man in the whole of Europe (see map opposite), and its purpose has never been discovered. Between 1777 and 1922 four attempts were made to solve the mystery by digging. A shaft was sunk from the top, and a hole burrowed from the side to the centre without anything being found to reveal its date or its builders. All that can be said with certainty is that the Hill was there before the Romans made their road past its foot; for when they reached the Hill they looped it round the base, which they would not have done if the Hill had not been there first.

Before leaving the great prehistoric monuments of Wiltshire we must finish the story of Stonehenge, which is in some ways more marvellous than that of any other ancient site.

As we have seen, in its earliest form, a ditch and bank 320 feet across were constructed by New Stone Age and Beaker tribes. The Aubrey Holes were dug and used for mysterious ceremonies which we can hardly guess at. Certainly some of them were used, perhaps a little later, for the burial of the ashes of the dead, and the site became a tribal cemetery. Four to five hundred years later a Food Vessel tribe, warlords of Wessex, and descendants of the Peterborough Folk, put up a group of stone circles and horseshoe settings near the centre of the older monument. Many of the stones were carefully shaped. The larger ones are sarsens, to be found in plenty on the Marlborough Downs, three miles west of Avebury; some of the smaller ones are of bluestone from the Prescelly Hills in west Wales which, as I explained earlier, had formed part of a stone circle with lintels, perhaps at the western end of the cursus. The chips of bluestone found in and near that point indicate that they were reshaped there before they were re-erected as part of the present Stonehenge.

Starting from the centre of the monument we have the altar-stone, which is of Welsh sandstone, unlike all the others used in the temple. It may once have stood upright like the rest. Round the altar-stone is a horseshoe of rocks from Wales. They face towards the Heelstone in the centre of the Avenue to the north-east. The plan on p. 50 will help you here.

If one stands by the altar-stone on midsummer morning, the sun is seen to rise above the Heelstone. Next after the bluestone horseshoe comes a larger one built of sarsens. These are arranged as five trilithons ('three-stones'), each with two uprights and a third sarsen as a lintel across the top of the other two (Pl. 5). Next again, moving outwards from the centre, is a circle of bluestones, and outside these a ring of great sarsens, originally thirty in number, with a lintel stone reaching from the middle of the top of each upright to the middle of the next. These lintels once formed an unbroken line right round the circle. They are held in place by mortice and tenon joints accurately carved in the stone. The use of these joints indicates that the builders were accustomed to working in wood and that they applied woodworking methods to stone.

Outside this wonderful circle is a double series of holes, in some of which Iron Age pottery as well as chips of bluestone were found. They therefore belong to a much later date than the rest of Stonehenge. These Y and Z holes, as they are called, may once have held timber or stone uprights, though there was not the slightest indication of either when they were excavated. Like so much else about Stonehenge they remain a mystery. Last of all, the outermost circle, just inside the ditch, consists of the Aubrey Holes, now marked by blocks of chalk.

This is such a complicated site that it may help you to understand it better if I sum up. In its earliest form (about 1850 B.C.) of ditch, bank, and Aubrey Holes, and perhaps a central timber monument like Woodhenge, it belongs to the very end of the New Stone Age, to the Peterborough and Grooved-Ware people. The stone structures, largely as we now see them, were probably the work of the Wessex warriors (about 1400 B.C.). In its last prehistoric phase of use the Belgae took it over, just before the arrival of the Roman legions in A.D. 43, and it is possible that the Druids presided at ceremonies there until the Romans drove them away.

The question is often asked how Stonehenge was built, and I shall try to answer it as far as I can. First of all we must not forget that ancient man had no railways, or surfaced roads, no large ships or cranes, no steel cables or hydraulic jacks for lifting heavy weights. Yet some of the stones had to be carried from afar, and though they weigh many tons each, they had to be lifted by some means into position.

The bluestones from Wales must have been dragged along a track from which the worst unevennesses had been removed. Each stone was placed on a sledge or, more probably, on rollers made from the trunks of young trees; and then, with men and oxen hauling on ropes made of hide, and others pushing from behind, the stones lumbered jerkily forward. There must have been some good teamwork in rushing from the rear to the front with those rollers that the stone had passed over so that each might be used again and again. This heavy task of haulage, uphill and down, must have been necessary for about twenty miles from the Prescelly Hills to the nearest stretch of water on Milford Haven. There the wooden rollers could be made into rafts and the stones paddled to a safe anchorage near the open sea.

There may have been a long wait then until fair weather set in. Steering these heavy, shapeless craft in any sort of wind would have been very difficult. Once clear of Milford Haven the great Atlantic rollers must have pitched the rafts about unmercifully. But, if the route were to St Ives Bay in south-west Cornwall, an open-sea crossing of over one hundred miles was necessary. An alternative route up the Bristol Channel and along the Bristol Avon and the little River Biss to near Trowbridge would still have left another difficult overland haulage of over twenty miles, much of it uphill.

Taking it that the longer route was used, we should have to imagine the log rafts becoming rollers again to move the stones the four miles across Cornwall from the Hayle estuary to near Penzance. From there a long coasting voyage round the Lizard and many other stormy points had to be made for at least two hundred miles until the other Avon was reached at Hengistbury Head, on the coast of Hampshire. Then the rafts had to be paddled upstream against the current for about thirty-five miles.

From the Avon at West Amesbury for a distance of one and a half miles, as far as the north-east segment of Stonehenge, there runs an avenue of which only the part near the standing stones is still normally visible. The rest of it can only be seen at times from the air. Up this gentle slope the stones were finally dragged. The avenue divides, one branch leading to the Avon and another to the cursus. Once the stones had arrived, holes were dug at points carefully marked out, and one side of each hole was sloped towards the bottom so that the stone would slide into place. With a great hauling on thongs of hide and rhythmic chanting, each stone was pushed and pulled until it was upright, and then packing stones, chalk rubble, and earth were rammed round the base to keep the stone firmly in position.

To get a lintel into position ramps of earth may have been built on one side of the two upright stones. The lintel stone could then be hauled and pushed up the slope of the ramp until it was nearly in place across the top. The task of fitting the stones together was completed with levers and stone hammers. Last of all, the earthen ramp could be taken away. It is possible that similar ramps were used to get all of the larger stones into an upright position.

Stonehenge, unlike Avebury and other circles, has carefully hewn rocks. Not only had the joints to be carved, but the lintels were cut with a curve on the inside face so that each formed a segment of a circle. No metal tools were used for the carving; flint chisels and large stone hammers, many of which have been found on the site, were the only implements that could have been employed.

When we consider the enormous labour involved in digging the Avebury ditch, years of work for many workmen with antler-picks, shovels from the bones of oxen, and wicker baskets instead of wheelbarrows; when we look at Silbury Hill and its millions of basketfuls of soil and chalk, and all the mighty labour of Stonehenge – the string of seventy rafts pitching in the Atlantic swell, the haulage of bluestones from Wales and sarsens from north Wiltshire, and the building of the ramps – when we think of all these heavy tasks, veritable labours of Hercules, we begin to realize how important these sacred monuments were to prehistoric men.

Salisbury Plain was the truly central region of prehistoric England. Towards it came hill-top tracks from almost every point of the compass, as you can see from the map on p. 86, and along these highways came people to witness the midsummer ceremonies or to bury their dead in the many barrows that are still to be seen all over the Plain. And many more have disappeared century by century as the plough took in ever more land for cultivation.

Yet elsewhere in Britain there are lesser circles of stones, though these are not usually surrounded by ditch and bank like Avebury and Stonehenge. As far as we know the smaller circles were built in the Early Bronze Age, but often they continued to be used as burial places in later prehistoric times. Arbor Low near Youlgreave in north Derbyshire has, in fact, a surrounding ditch, but the stones are lying flat on the ground round the inside edge of the ditch and overlap the two entrance causeways. It looks as though the stone circle was added to the earlier henge monument.

Stone circles without a ditch can be seen at Stanton Drew in Somerset, near Little Salkeld and near Keswick in Cumberland, at Great Rollright in Oxfordshire, and in many places in the stone regions of the north and west of Britain.

These great monuments show, above all, that ancient peoples could organize themselves into teams to undertake vast works which they thought were for the good of all; and we shall see later, when we talk of the great hill-forts and running earthworks, that tribes of the early Iron Age and of the late Roman period could also join together to complete a task which they hoped would give them greater safety from their enemies.

Henge Monuments still to be Seen

(a) Those with a single entrance: the earliest Stonehenge, nine miles north of Salisbury (plan on p. 50 and Pl. 5); Woodhenge, also nine miles north of Salisbury; Arminghall, two miles south-east of Norwich; Gorsey Bigbury, four miles north-west of Priddy, Somerset; a site discovered from the air at Stratford Hills, seven and a half miles north-east of Colchester, Essex; Mayburgh, one mile south of Penrith, Cumberland; five sites, now destroyed, at Dorchester, Oxfordshire; Maumbury Rings, just outside Dorchester, Dorset, altered by the Romans into an arena; Castle Dykes, near Aysgarth in the North Riding of Yorkshire; and the Stripple Stones, seven miles north-east of Bodmin, Cornwall.

(b) Those with two opposite entrances: Avebury (four entrances), twelve miles south of Swindon (map, p. 58, and Pl. 4); Arbor Low, three miles west of Youlgreave, Derbyshire; Bull Ring, Doveholes, three miles north-east of Buxton, Derbyshire; Westwell, two miles south-west of Burford, Oxfordshire (slight traces); Durrington Walls, near Woodhenge, Wiltshire; Fargo Plantation (very small), near Stonehenge; the Knowlton circles (map, p. 56), Dorset; and one 350 yards east of Eggardon hill-fort, ten miles west of Dorchester, Dorset.

(*c*) Those with two ditches and a bank between them, and two entrances: three circles on Thornborough Moor, five miles north of Ripon; one on Hutton Moor, nearly three miles north-east of Ripon and another the same distance west of Ripon on Cana Moor. The largest of the henges at Dorchester, Oxfordshire, also belonged to this group.

(*d*) There are probable henges at Staden Low, near the Bull Ring (see (*b*) above); at Thornhaugh, eight miles west of Peterborough in Northamptonshire; at Budbury, Bradford-on-Avon, Wiltshire; at Marden, north Wiltshire; at Mount Pleasant, one mile east of Dorchester, Dorset; at Castlewich, Callington, Cornwall; at Coupland, about a mile north of Wooler, Northumberland; and on Berwick Down, Maddington, Wiltshire. Some of these were only recently discovered.

(*e*) Stone circles may be seen on Bodmin Moor and near Penzance, Cornwall; on Dartmoor and Exmoor, Devon; in the Welsh mountains and on the mountains of north-west England.

(*f*) Besides the cursus monuments near Stonehenge, at Gussage, Dorset (map, p. 56), and within Maiden Castle, Dorset, others, which can be seen only from the air, occur at Benson, Drayton, and Dorchester, Oxfordshire.

In Museums

There are models of Stonehenge, restored, in the museums at Salisbury and Devizes.

Note on Stonehenge: In 1953 remarkable new discoveries were made. On some of the great sarsens there are carvings of Irish axes and Mycenean daggers. They are visible only at certain times of the day when the sun is in a position favourable for casting shadows in the hollows of these very worn-down carvings. It is thought that a Mycenean trading post may have been established not far away beside the river Avon at the end of the ceremonial Avenue leading from Stonehenge. The Y and Z holes, in which Belgic pottery was found, are now known to be much earlier in date. They had been dug to take upright stones and then, after a change of plan, they were left open to fill in naturally. The Belgic and Roman potsherds found in them had been drawn down through the soil by earthworms.

Durrington Walls: The laying of a pipe through this 'henge' revealed dwelling sites of the Grooved-Ware people who had had a part in the building of several of the 'henge' monuments. It is now known, also, that the Stonehenge Avenue did not divide into two parts and experiments have shown that there was a better way of raising the great stones than by the use of earthen ramps.

3: Early and Middle Bronze Age Peoples

ALREADY in the New Stone Age the Windmill Hill Folk, who had originally come from the Mediterranean lands, and the Peterborough Folk from northern Europe, had begun to intermarry. Some pottery from Whitehawk camp near Brighton and from Easton Down, Wiltshire, shows the mixed fashions of the two tribes. The Grooved-Ware and the Peterborough Folk had also intermarried with the Middle Stone Age people, who had survived in Britain from the end of the last Ice Age. Yet other streams of people may have merged with them; for certainly the new mixed peoples show in their possessions that they had been influenced by tribes from northern Ireland and by the western tribes who had built the great stone tombs. With all these the Beaker overlords gradually mixed, and a new way of life grew up.

The new people are best known from their pots, called 'food vessels', which they buried with their dead. In Scotland and north-eastern England many of their burials have been discovered in stone cists (box-like graves made of stone slabs) (see Pl. 3b). The pots found in them show especially the influence of the Peterborough and Beaker peoples, though the broad-headed skulls of many of the skeletons indicate that the Beaker Folk made up a large part of the Food Vessel peoples. Owing to what may have been a fresh invasion from Brittany into Wessex about 1550 B.C., it is difficult to understand what happened to these peoples in southern Britain. At any

5½"

Middle Bronze Age
Yorkshire food vessel

rate, from Dorset along the chalk hills of Wiltshire, Berkshire, and the Chiltern Hills to round the Wash, their urns are found, but not in the great numbers that are known from the Peak district, Lincolnshire, and farther to the north-east.

Some of the food vessels from Yorkshire are marked on the base with a pattern like the grain of wood. Some beakers, especially the few with handles, have this pattern too. Both these kinds of pots were probably easily-made substitutes for wooden vessels, and they serve to remind us that the many wooden objects in everyday use in ancient times have very seldom survived in Britain, though there may have been a greater use of wood and basketry than of clay for holding and storing food and drink.

The Yorkshire people, and those of Northumberland, lived mostly by keeping cattle and by hunting; but they also grew corn, or perhaps bought it from other tribes who did, for the casts of barley grains have been found on some of their pots. They also inherited the trading connexions of the Peterborough tribes, and grew rich through their commerce. With their wealth they were able to buy beautiful bead necklaces of jet, and gold ornaments and earrings. Although stone was still used for many tools, they could afford to buy bronze goods from Ireland, where a great export trade had grown up based on the metal-ores to be found there. In fact, the Food Vessel tribes bought

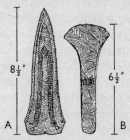

Middle Bronze Age: (A) Bronze dagger, Camerton, Soms; (B) Bronze axe, Normanton, Wilts

Irish bronze axes, small daggers, and halberds. Their graves are often found beside the prehistoric highways along which they traded these goods; and it was probably the same people who carried similar bronze weapons to Denmark and north Germany, where they have been discovered in recent times.

Not all the Food Vessel people were buried unburned; some were certainly cremated. In East Yorkshire, where there are many hundreds of their barrows on the Cleveland Hills, one in five of the burials was burned. The burial, burned or unburned, may be in a cist or in a shallow pit, and it may be covered with a barrow or cairn. Sometimes the mourners dug a shallow ditch under the barrow or erected a ring of wooden posts before adding the earth or stones to the mound. In other parts of northern England a cairn may cover three or four burials. In Yorkshire one cairn might be used in turn by New Stone Age, Beaker, Food Vessel, and later tribes for the interment of their dead. The same spot continued to be regarded as a holy place for many centuries.

Yet a further custom is sometimes found. The body was sometimes buried at full length (and not crouched as with the Beaker Folk) in an oak trunk that had been split and hollowed out for the purpose. The same custom was in use later in Denmark and Holland. Some of these oak coffins are shaped at each end like a ship; and one Yorkshire burial was actually put in a dug-out canoe. They show clearly that trade could be carried on by water in the Bronze Age, and the boat-shaped coffins may represent a belief in a voyage to the next world after death, such as was held by the ancient Egyptians and by the Romans. Perhaps it was the bodies of chiefs who had commanded distant trading expeditions that were honoured by burial in a boat-coffin.

On the Downlands of southern England the Wessex people are found instead of the Food Vessel tribes. They were a ruling class like the Beaker people whom they replaced, and, like them also, grew wealthy and could buy luxuries from far and near. We cannot be sure whether they came over from Brittany or whether they were clever native merchants who grew rich quickly through the hard work of the tribes they had conquered: the herdsmen, farmers, and flint-miners who were already living in the region. The Wessex folk obtained metal from Ireland, amber from the Baltic coasts (see figure B below), and beads from as far away as the Mediterranean. And they employed smiths who used new methods of shaping bronze by casting; the old way was to hammer it into shape while it was hot. There were gold-smiths, too, who covered boxes and buttons and other objects with thin sheets of gold from Ireland. Carpenters worked with a simple lathe, and though their wooden products have not survived, cups of shale (a soft stone) have been found in the graves of Wessex chiefs.

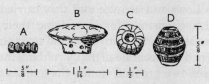

Middle Bronze Age: (A) Segmented faience (glazed earthenware) bead, Lake, Wilts; (B) Amber pommel; (C) Bead, Manton, Wilts; (D) Lignite bead banded with gold

The Mediterranean beads (see figure A above) found in twenty-five Wessex graves are of unusual interest; they help us to arrive at the first reliable date in British prehistory. They were imported ready-made from the eastern Mediterranean, and the most exact parallel to them is seen in beads from an Egyptian grave that can be safely dated to about 1400 B.C. But other considerations, too complicated to talk about here, make a date around 1550 B.C. a reliable one for the beginning of the Wessex culture in southern Britain.

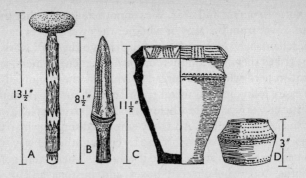

Middle Bronze Age: (A) Sceptre with head of shale, Normanton, Wilts; (B) Bronze spearhead; (C) Cinerary urn, Soham, Cambs; (D) Pygmy cup, Lake, Wilts

The Wessex warrior chieftains, like the Beaker men, were armed with bows and arrows; and they carried a bronze dagger and a whetstone for sharpening their weapons. Arrows were still headed with flint, and their shafts could be straightened for accurate flight by rubbing them up and down between two grooved stones. Sometimes these warriors were armed with a bronze-headed spear (B above); sometimes with a double-edged stone battle-axe rather like that shown on p. 42. The chiefs might carry sceptres a foot long (A above), with shale or stone tops set with gold studs. A few of them were buried with the later kind of pottery known as cinerary urns (that is, urns for holding the ashes of a cremation) (C above); others have a very small vessel of clay (D above), shale, or amber which might be in one of several forms. About a quarter of the Wessex chiefs were buried in a crouched position like the Beaker people; the remainder were cremated. Burials have been found in wooden coffins or simply on planks, and a few were placed in hollow tree-trunks like some of the northern Food Vessel chiefs. Later in the Middle Bronze Age there was even more similarity in the customs of all the many tribes up and down the country, and this is the one period of prehistory when such a similarity existed.

Almost all of the objects mentioned in the last few paragraphs may be seen in museums, but the burial mounds of the Wessex chiefs still exist in many places on the open downland of southern England. Some were buried in bell barrows, in which a space of flat earth is left untouched between the pile of soil and the encircling ditch; others, after cremation, were placed under a very small mound with a large flat space between the hummock and the surrounding ditch and bank. This second kind is called a disc barrow.

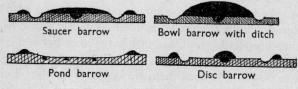

Saucer barrow   Bowl barrow with ditch

Pond barrow   Disc barrow

Types of Prehistoric barrows

Both kinds can be seen in the regions round Stonehenge and Avebury (see above and p. 45).

In Cornwall similar customs are found. Burials are often in cists covered by cairns, and in one of them a gold cup was found which is very much like cups from graves in Mycenae in southern Greece. The goods placed with the remains of the dead of this time, in the south-western counties, south Wales, and Yorkshire, are sometimes similar to those buried with the Wessex chiefs. They probably show that other tribal leaders could also become wealthy and buy costly treasures and then proudly bury them with their dead. It may well be that the Prescelly stones were brought to Stonehenge to make the great monument in its present form by these rich and powerful Wessex lords; but the stones have not yet given up all their secrets, and we cannot be sure.

All this while the tribes subject to the Wessex lords, a mixture of the Beaker Folk and the old Peterborough people, were growing more powerful as merchants and traders, as well as by farming. They spread from southern England all over Britain, and even into Ireland and to the Dutch and north French coasts. From about 1400 B.C. onwards their tall urns of coarse clay (see p. 72, C) begin to become common. They were developed from the food vessels, and like them they were used for containing the ashes of the dead. They show differences in shape and in the patterns marked on them according to the area in which they were made. And as time went on these cinerary urns gradually underwent various changes in their form and decoration, so that it is possible to distinguish between earlier and later varieties of them.

The people who used them are known as the Urn Folk, and like the Wessex chiefs they often buried their dead under barrows. In the North, however, the custom was different. There, a number of urns may be buried together in cemeteries with hardly any sign of a mound over them. From about 1200 B.C. the practice of burying corpses ceased altogether; cremation had become the sole custom everywhere. Bell barrows (see page 45) continued to be built as tombs, but other kinds were made too. In the Pond Cairn at Coity, Glamorgan, where coal and barley were found by the excavators, the urn containing the chief's ashes was first covered by a pile of stones and then with turves. Round the whole barrow a low wall was built to keep all in place.

Older stone circles, or new ones specially put up for the purpose, were sometimes used for burial places. In the Lake district the stones occasionally have spiral patterns carved on them. At Bleasdale, ten miles north of Preston, Lancashire (map, p. 86), the ashes of an Urn chief were buried in a pit four feet deep, round which there stood eleven great oak trunks set in a low mound. Around the mound the mourners dug a ditch and lined it with poles cut from birch trees. A part of what should have been ditch was left undug to serve as an entrance to the central enclosure. Outside all this they set another ring of posts, placed close together but with an entrance gap not quite in line with the one to the inner enclosure.

Sometimes as many as thirty of these cremation burials are unearthed together, occasionally in rows or circles but without anything on the surface to show their position. Not all the ashes are contained in pots; some are merely placed in a hole in the ground and covered over with earth. Other urns have been found by themselves at the centre of wide circular banks, like early henge monuments but without an entrance through the outer ring. Various other burial arrangements were in use under large or small barrows or cairns, and especially under those that had been built by earlier peoples of the New Stone and Bronze Ages. Burials in cists were especially common, and a number of these graves are to be seen, particularly on Dartmoor (Pl. 3b).

Few objects, such as weapons or ornaments, are ever discovered with Urn Folk burials; occasionally a narrow knife, a flint arrow-head, a stone axe-head, or a mace is found. Beads, including some from Egypt like those treasured by the Wessex chiefs (see p. 71), may occur in a few graves of the North.

Because they burned their dead we know less about these people than about some earlier ones, for it was not usual for them to bury the dead person's possessions with his ashes in the urn. His valuables were probably destroyed with his corpse on the funeral pyre. Another result of the custom of burning corpses was that a great deal of wood had to be used for each pyre. It had to be brought from the fringes of the vast forests that covered much of Britain throughout pre-history. The grazing of cattle since New Stone Age times must already have begun to push back the margins of these forests, and the custom of cremation almost certainly speeded up the process and enlarged the areas cleared of woodland.

Since we know from the increasing numbers of burials that the population was steadily growing larger, this expansion of open country on which food could be grown must have been very welcome. But more farming meant an increase in the number of cattle. This would also help to speed up the process of forest clearance, for by pasturing the cattle on the edges of the wooded regions, and just inside them, the farmers prevented new trees growing from seed; cattle crop them off before the stems become too hard. So you see, the burning of corpses and the grazing of cattle together helped to provide more food, especially meat and milk from the cattle and corn from the newly cleared fields. This process of destroying the forests went on steadily, sometimes faster, sometimes more slowly, until about the reign of Queen Elizabeth I. From the seventh century after Christ, when the English had become securely settled in this country, the process grew ever faster.

We know very little about the lives of the Urn Folk, but at least we can be sure that they grew barley, wheat, and flax because their urns sometimes show the impress of these grains. But although corn was still grown, stock-breeding and hunting remained the easiest means of obtaining food. With the increase of population there was a move on to poorer soils, especially on to the moors of western and northern England. Large cattle-pens surrounded by walls (now tumbled down) or by earthen banks that were once crowned by high fences, can still be seen on the Somerset hills and

Berkshire downs. On the bad soils of Dartmoor, too, there are many of these large 'pounds', sometimes with stone hut-circles nearby or inside them (see p. 79 and Pl. 6a). Tiny irregular fields, too small to plough, are sometimes to be seen in the same locality as the pounds. They could only have been cultivated with the hoe.

If you visit Trowlesworthy Warren, two miles north-east of the village of Shaugh Prior and just beside the river Plym on the south-western borders of Dartmoor, you can see eight little fields and forty hut-circles, besides several other kinds of Bronze Age stone monuments. On Standon Hill, three miles south-east of Lydford, there are over seventy hut-circles on the dry western-facing slope which goes down to the river Tavy, and with them are fifteen small cultivation plots. There are numerous other places on Dartmoor and Bodmin Moor where similar groups of ancient remains may be seen. On page 98 you will find diagrams of some of these sites.

There are fields also on the Cleveland Moors in Yorkshire, from which the smaller stones have been picked and cast to the edges. But the plots are still scattered with larger boulders that would have prevented ploughing with oxen. On poor lowland soils in Cheshire, on the fells of the Lake District, and on the moors of the Pennine Chain, traces of the Urn Folk have been found. Probably in these poorer regions they lived chiefly by keeping goats and pigs, especially pigs; and on the borders of the moorlands where the forests began, goats and pigs, more than other domestic animals, would quite quickly destroy the woodland by preventing the growth of young trees to replace the old ones as they died.

Some of the remains of fields and huts mentioned above may possibly belong to earlier or later people, but most archaeologists think that they were made by the Urn Folk.

At any rate the British climate from about 2000 to 700 B.C. was more favourable to settlement on the high moorland plateaux because in that period, which is also mainly that of the Bronze Age, it was warmer and drier. Before 2000 and after 700 the growing of crops would have been very difficult owing to the greater rainfall and the lack of sunshine, and apart from this difficulty, conditions would have made life very wretched for all who were condemned to dwell on these wet uplands. It is a fact that in the wetter periods of our climate, before and after the Bronze Age, moorland regions were almost deserted; certainly there is little to be seen dating from the New Stone Age or Early Iron Age, and even to-day our moors are almost bare of villages and hamlets, or even of solitary cottages. Round Pound, Kestor, near Chagford, and on the driest edge of Dartmoor, is now known to be of the Early Iron Age, but no other site of this period has yet been found on the Moors (Pl. 7a).

The Urn Folk knew how to weave woollen cloth, for some of it was found in one of their urns at Coniston in Lancashire; and the impressions of flax grains on their pots suggest that they could weave linen. These were women's tasks, as was the making of pots. For the men hunting and farming were the main occupations.

The hut-circles on Dartmoor had stone walls about five feet high, and it is likely that the roof, made of branches and turves, rose to a point in the middle where it was supported by a stout post. The hole for such a support can still be seen on some of the hut sites right in the centre of the floor. Near it is a large flat stone on which a peat fire burned, and close to one of these hearths a crock was found with a pot-boiler beside it. The cooking arrangements were sometimes completed by a cooking-hole about fifteen inches deep. To one side of the hut is a low stone platform used as a seat by day and a bed by night.

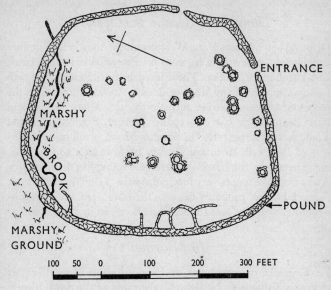

ENTRANCE

MARSHY

BROOK

MARSHY GROUND

POUND

100 50 0   100   200   300 FEET

Grimspound, Dartmoor; the pound and hut-circles

Some of the huts stand alone: usually several are situated close together. At Grimspound (Pl. 6a), three miles north-east of Postbridge, the pound wall encloses the site of twenty huts, each between ten and fifteen feet across. Some, with wide entrances, may have housed cattle, and the animals could be kept near the huts by the long surrounding wall. This was formerly about five feet high, sufficient to keep the cattle from straying. It is this enclosing wall that is the actual 'pound', of which many may be seen on Dartmoor, especially near Postbridge. This is a region well worth visiting if ever you are on holiday at one of the south Devon coastal resorts; but you should be ready for some rough walking if you are to see more than a few of the well-visited sites near the main roads.

Things to be Seen in the Open Air

Disc and bell barrows of the Wessex culture, mostly in Wiltshire and Dorset. A few disc barrows on Petersfield Heath, Hants, and Lambourne, Berks. The Bleasdale burial circle in north Lancashire. The many kinds of Bronze Age monuments on the moors of the South-west and North-east. Many Beaker and later Bronze Age barrows round Wetton, Staffordshire and Youlgreave, Derbyshire. On Stanton Moor, seven miles south-east of Bakewell, there are seventy barrows in a square mile, made mostly by the Urn Folk. A few are rather like disc barrows. Away from the moors very few house sites of the Middle Bronze Age are known, probably because the huts were made of skins stretched over a wicker frame. Stonehenge in its present form.

In Museums

Food vessels, cinerary urns, and various kinds of smaller pots that were sometimes buried with the ashes of the dead. Bronze weapons and implements. Stone double-headed battle-axes and arrow straighteners. Mediterranean beads.

Bronzesmiths and Merchants

During the Bronze Age Britain and Ireland became centres of manufacture doing a brisk trade by exporting tools and weapons. Only a few of these objects have been found with burials. Perhaps bronze was thought too valuable to be lost in this way, though ancient peoples often buried their greatest treasures with the dead.

As it is, our knowledge of late Bronze Age weapons has been mostly gained from 'hoards'. Towards the end of the Age especially, travelling tradesmen who were both merchants and smiths went about the country collecting broken and worn implements for melting down. With the metal obtained in this way they could cast new goods for sale. The stock of scrap metal carried by these merchants was very valuable, and if they encountered danger, and they had the time, they would bury their hoard of stock out of sight in the earth, and return for it when the danger was past. For some the danger did not pass, and they never returned to dig up their precious hoards.

We can easily imagine that if the merchant had had a very profitable trip and had collected a greater weight of bronze scrap than he could carry comfortably, he might bury some of it and look forward to an early return to such a profitable region. But sometimes he did not return, and the blunt and broken tools remained in the earth until found by chance in modern times. Sometimes his stock was lost as he was fording a river. Perhaps it was deeper than he expected and he was swept away, with his load pulling him under the water until he was drowned. Sometimes a boat would capsize and the hoard be lost in deep water. It might then only see the light of day again when it was sorted out from the mud brought up from the river-bed by a modern dredger. In marshy country the merchant might be caught far from a village as night fell and perish. The acid soil would dissolve his bones during three thousand years and leave only his stock of bronze to tell of the tragedy.

Moving on from place to place, having no tribe of his own, he would trade his new stock for a greater weight of scrap metal, and for food, drink, and shelter. When his stock of new goods ran low he would melt down the scrap into large cakes of bronze like those often found with the hoards. A solid cake of metal was easier to carry than a jangling mass of blunt and worn implements. Some of the cakes would be remelted and cast into new tools for sale to his customers.

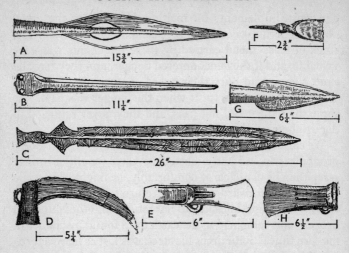

Late Bronze Age objects: (A) Bronze spearhead, Congleton hoard, Cheshire; (B) Bronze rapier, Maentwrog hoard, Merioneth; (C) Bronze sword, the Thames; (D) Bronze socketed sickle, Winterbourne Monkton, Wilts; (E) Bronze palstave (axe fitted on a split haft and bound with cords), Nettleham hoard, Lincs; (F) Bronze chisel, Oldbury Hill, Calne, Wilts; (G) Bronze spearhead, Guilsfield hoard, Montgom.; (H) Bronze axe, Llyn Fawr hoard, Glam.

These hoards can tell us a surprising amount about the kinds of weapons and tools in use during the Bronze Age (see above). When different types are found together in one hoard we know that those types were all in use at about the same time. And if the find-spots of the hoards are marked on maps, we can discover the trade routes of the period. We can see how these old traders followed the trackways along the hills and crossed the rivers at particular fords. The many weapons drawn up from the deeper parts of rivers when they are being dredged makes it clear that much trade went by water. And the finds of British weapons across the North Sea show that the merchants were willing to face the dangers of storm and shipwreck in their search for customers.

To simple Bronze Age villagers, who never went far out of sight of their own huts, these travelling smiths, with their strange tales of distant places, must have been welcome guests. And they were very useful, too; for bronze could be bought only from them. Flint tools, which were still in use for many purposes, could not be used for some of the jobs that could be tackled only with a bronze edge. But although the smiths were welcome for their stories and for their stock of goods, they must have been feared, too. They had knowledge of so many things unknown to the villagers; and it must have seemed wizardry when they produced new tools from old, and even sometimes in a quite different shape. Besides, they had no tribe and no home, and seemed to come from nowhere and pass on to nowhere. The villagers must have felt towards the smiths as country people until recent times felt towards the gypsies: they envied them and were suspicious of them and feared them.

Daggers, spearheads, swords, rapiers, scabbards, axes of several kinds, great round shields, chisels, and gouges of this period were all finely made. Between the Early and Late Bronze Ages many gradual changes of form and fashion can be seen in the design of the implements. In general they increased in usefulness as time went on; and in some types there was a saving in the amount of metal required without any loss of usefulness.

We have no knowledge of the methods used in mining the copper and tin for making bronze. There was plenty of copper in Ireland, and supplies could be had from Wales or Cumberland. Tin, in any quantity, could be got only in Cornwall. The ores of both metals were probably obtained from surface veins, perhaps worked back into a hillside, where that was possible. Gold was panned from the beds of Scottish and Irish streams and some from Ireland was exchanged for Cornish tin, a metal Ireland lacked but needed for alloying into bronze with her plentiful copper.

Another material exchanged for tin or for finished bronze goods was the amber found as beads or as pommels (see p. 71) in a number of Wessex graves. This precious substance is the fossilized gum from certain extinct kinds of pine trees, and was found chiefly on the Baltic shores of Jutland and perhaps a little of it on our own East Coast. Amber beads have been found in fourteen graves of the Wessex chiefs, together with the Egyptian faience (glazed earthenware) beads (see p. 71). This, and the fact that British weapons were sold all along the coasts of western and northern Europe, from Spain to Scandinavia, shows how wide the trading contacts of the time could be.

With the coming of iron to Britain some time after 500 B.C., the blacksmith put the bronzesmith out of business except in the remoter parts of the British Isles. Invaders from Holland who settled on Castle Hill, Scarborough, were well equipped with a fine assortment of bronze tools, weapons, and trinkets, but among their many possessions found in excavations was an iron pin, the oldest object of iron so far discovered in Britain. Their pottery, too, was of a kind usual among Iron Age tribes. At about the same time Late Bronze Age refugees from France, who settled on the Sussex downland at Plumpton Plain, near Brighton, had some edge tools of iron. None was actually recovered from their farmstead, but a whetstone for sharpening tools was unearthed, and chemists have been able to say with certainty that iron implements were sharpened against the stone, for traces of iron were found in its surface.

Once a knowledge of the use of iron had reached this country there was plenty of it to be mined, and its abundance made it much cheaper than bronze. It was also far more useful, because iron will keep a sharp edge for longer and can be used for jobs that would completely ruin a bronze tool; moreover, an iron edge can be easily re-sharpened, which bronze cannot.

Ancient Routes

Trade within Britain could be carried on only if there were routes that merchants could follow from customer to customer through the length and breadth of our island. The discovery of prehistoric trackways has added a great deal to our understanding of ancient peoples and of their intermixing, their trading, their routes of invasion, and their tribal movements after they had settled here.

No routes are known of which we can say with certainty, 'This came into use in the Bronze Age', or 'This was first trodden by New Stone Age man'. If, however, we notice that a track passes close to a number of long barrows at various points in its length, and that a causewayed camp stands near it at another point, we can say with little doubt that it was in use during the New Stone Age, if not before. And if, in addition, we know that New Stone Age tools or potsherds, or both, have been picked up on or near its course, then the probability becomes the stronger.

As it is very unlikely that the limestone uplands were ever deserted between New Stone Age times and the end of the Roman period, and as we know also that new invaders mixed with the tribes already here, we can usually conclude that a New Stone Age track continued in use almost until the coming of the Saxons. This is not always true, but likely exceptions are few. The most important exception is the Cotswold Hills, which had a considerable population in New Stone Age times but a small one in the Bronze Age. Yet even then the Hills continued to afford an easy forest-free route from south-west Britain through the Midlands to

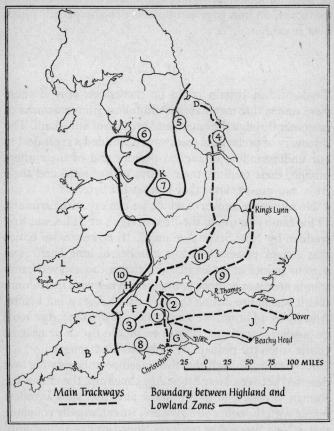

Ancient trackways: (1) Stonehenge; (2) Avebury; (3) Glastonbury; (4) Danes' Graves; (5) Thornborough circles; (6) Bleasdale; (7) Arbor Low; (8) Maiden Castle; (9) Wheathampstead; (10) Lydney; (11) Hunsbury

(A) Bodmin Moor; (B) Dartmoor; (C) Exmoor; (D) North Yorkshire Moors; (E) Yorkshire Wolds; (F) Mendip Hills; (G) New Forest; (H) Forest of Dean; (J) The Weald; (K) The Peak District

the coast in north-east Yorkshire, and finds of Bronze Age implements all along the Hills prove that men and trade continued to pass along them.

If you look at a map of modern England showing roads and railways you will see that they radiate from the area where the greatest numbers of people live, that is, London. A map of Britain before the Roman period (opposite) shows that all the main tracks led towards Salisbury Plain, to the neighbourhood of Stonehenge and Avebury, the region most thickly settled of any in prehistoric Britain.

Four great trunk routes existed. One began at Beachy Head in Sussex, and ran along the South Downs, past long barrows, flint mines, and several New Stone Age camps. It went on across the downs of Hampshire and on to Salisbury Plain. Another begins on the chalk cliffs above Dover, runs along the North Downs through Kent and Surrey, and crosses northern Hampshire on its way to Stonehenge. The third is longer. It starts near King's Lynn in northern Norfolk, goes southward to Thetford, near where it passes close to the flint mines at Grime's Graves, and then swings south-westward along the Chilterns. It goes over the Thames by any one of several fords near Goring, Oxfordshire, and then runs along the Berkshire downs and on into Wiltshire. From Thetford to Goring it has long been called the Icknield Way and in Berkshire it is known as the Ridgeway.

The fourth great track is the one that begins on the Cleveland Hills in north-east Yorkshire and crosses the North York Moors and the Wolds of the East Riding. South of the difficult crossing of the Humber it followed Lincoln Edge and then went on, bearing more and more to the south-westward through Leicestershire, Northamptonshire, Oxfordshire, and Gloucestershire. Beyond the Bristol Avon are ridges running south-west to link with the Mendip Hills. This route has been named the Jurassic Way, since for most of its length it runs along a band of limestone which occurs also in the Jura Mountains of eastern France. From the Gloucestershire section of the Jurassic Way there are several possible short routes to Salisbury Plain.

Besides these four trunk routes a minor one can be traced leading westward from the Plain to the Mendips; a second goes southward into north Dorset and then on to Cornwall; and a third makes for the south towards harbours at Poole and Christchurch. Like the four main routes these radiate from Salisbury Plain, but there are many lesser ones known along the hill-tops of Britain which served merely local needs; and even more are still to be traced by enthusiasts in the field.

Many ancient ways follow water-partings (that is, the higher ground from which the head-streams of rivers begin on both sides), and they wind backwards and forwards to avoid the tiny brooks and their marshy borders. But it is quite wrong to think that early man was frightened to get his feet wet. In fact, he must have spent many days of his life soaked to the skin over his whole body. In any case, the frequent finds of pottery, tools, weapons, and trinkets of every prehistoric period at fords shows that they were in constant use in ancient times and indeed almost to the present day in some parts of the country. But what early man did avoid were the marshy belts that must have occurred almost all along both banks of our rivers and brooks before mediaeval and modern drainage dried them out. Even to-day after a spell of rain the water meadows beside many streams are impassable.

In early times fords were not sought mainly because of their shallower water. The names sometimes given to them by our primitive Anglo-Saxon ancestors show that the depth of water was a matter of secondary importance. Deptford (*deep ford*) on the Roman Watling Street was a very important river crossing on the route from the Continent through Kent to London; and similar names occur in other counties with the same meaning. Durnford (*secret*, or *hidden*, *ford*) occurs with varying spellings in several counties, and implies that some of the crossings were so deep that the bottom of the ford could not be seen. It was not, then, the depth of water that mattered so much as that the approaches to the ford should not be marshy; and for this to be possible there had to be a gravel bank or spit, or higher, and so drier, ground, coming right down to the water's edge on both sides of the crossing; and this is not often found except in chalk country. The rarity of fords in some parts of the country caused tracks to converge on them from a wide area.

Another mistake is to imagine that prehistoric tracks were normally a few yards wide like modern roads. Aerial photographs reveal that in places the Icknield Way was as much as a quarter of a mile broad. A photograph from the air of Therfield Heath, near Royston, Hertfordshire, shows tracks spreading wide across the open chalk downs. Some of the tracks seen in the air-photo were no doubt made by the hooves of pack-horses in mediaeval and early modern times, but they were very likely following paths that had first been trodden out by prehistoric man and his beasts.

These tracks spread so widely because the most direct path was quickly churned up in wet weather and a parallel track on drier ground was easier to follow. In the longer wet spells of autumn, winter, and spring, when there was little sun to dry the soil, many such parallel paths would have been made. If you think for a moment of the state of the ground at any time of the year at the entrance to a busy farm-yard, or along a much-used country footpath, you will easily understand what I mean.

Wherever ancient routes leave the valleys for the hills it is worth looking for the fanning-out of the tracks towards the top of the ascent. Often there is a modern metalled road taking the same route but seeking an easier gradient than the old one. Where for one reason or another the track could not spread, as for instance on a local route from a watering-place (a well or a brook) up to a prehistoric farmstead, hamlet, or hill-fort, a hollow-way is formed. Countless feet of men and beasts for many centuries have worn down the surface sometimes for twenty feet into the hillside. First of all the turf covering was worn away, then the subsoil was broken up and washed downhill by the first heavy shower. As the track got deeper it formed a gutter for rainwater, which became a powerful stream and cut the channel still deeper. In very many places on the steep slopes of the downs of southern England these hollow-ways may be seen, though not all of them may be so ancient.

The wheel was probably not known in Britain before the Late Bronze Age, when harness for attaching animals to wheeled vehicles began to come into use. From the Iron Age survive many beautifully designed and wrought trappings for horses. We know from the writings of Julius Caesar that the Britons were very skilled in their handling of chariots. All that survives of them to-day are the iron tyres, the bronze band that went round the naves of the wheels, bronze linch-pins, and horse-trappings and harness. What is important at the moment, however, is that wheeled vehicles were in use in the Early Iron Age. Generally, all the wooden parts have long ago rotted away and disappeared, so that if there were any wagons made solely of wood, only a lucky find in peat (which preserves wood and other vegetable substances) is likely to give us any information about them.

Such a find was made in the Glastonbury lake village, of which I shall have more to say later. It consisted of part of an axle-box and a spoke. Originally the wheel had twelve spokes and stood nearly three feet high. Wagons could not be bought from a factory but were made in the village itself, as an unfinished part of a wheel showed. Wagons and carts continued to be built by village craftsmen until quite recently; indeed, there may be a few wheelwrights' shops still working in remote parts of the country even to-day.

For long-distance trade, goods were no doubt often carried on the backs of men or beasts, for few tracks could have been suitable for wheeled vehicles except for short distances. Sledges, like the one found in a Beaker warrior's grave at Dorchester-on-Thames, were used too, but on rough tracks their period of usefulness must have been brief. It must never be forgotten that properly surfaced roads were not known in this country until the coming of the Romans. In Late Bronze Age times short lengths of causeway over marshy ground were made by putting down brushwood and logs. Such causeways have been found in the Fens of Cambridgeshire and the Isle of Ely, in one case with scraps of Bronze Age pottery; and another was unearthed that joined the Iron Age Glastonbury lake village with dry land.

Boats must have been commonly used from New Stone Age times onwards, for the many prehistoric invasions of Britain could have been made only by sea. A number of dug-out canoes has been discovered in the beds of streams or in what were once marshes, lakes, or the courses of rivers. They vary in length from eight to nearly fifty feet, and they differ, too, in shape and construction. Almost all seem to have been propelled by a paddle wielded at the stern, and this must have served also as a rudder for steering.

Apart from dug-out canoes, coracles made of wickerwork with skin stretched across it were also in use. The same kind of boat was until recently being made in Wales, Ireland, and Scotland; and it must have been the larger curragh, of similar construction, that Caesar saw at sea off the southeast coast of England. The remains of a coracle were found

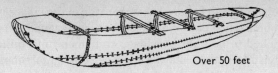

Over 50 feet

The Early Iron Age. Sewn wooden carvel-built boat,
North Ferriby, Yorks

at South Ferriby on the Lincolnshire side of the Humber; and at North Ferriby, on the opposite shore, a boat made of planks sewn together was unearthed. Now there are several remarkable conclusions that may be drawn from the discoveries of these boats. Their precise age is unknown, but the difference in their build suggests that they sank at widely separated times, probably on occasions when the fierce tidal wave, called the eagre, swept up the Humber from the sea.

The two Ferribys stand close to the points where the Humber breaks through the Jurassic Way, and it is tempting to think that the two craft were ferry-boats that linked the broken ends of that great trunk route. Fording the Humber there would have been very dangerous. The last strange fact is that Ferriby means 'village, or farm, by the ferry'. The two names cannot be proved to have been in use before they were written down in the Domesday Survey of A.D. 1086; but it is likely that the villages had been founded long before that date and that a ferry had crossed the broad Humber with little interruption right back through Danish and Anglo-Saxon times. The Roman ferry was a little upstream, at Brough on the line of a main Roman road; and the two boats suggest that prehistoric man made the crossing at the same points as his Norman successors. Thus a great span of past time is covered by this river crossing.

We have spoken about prehistoric routes, wagons, and boats; now for a little while we must think about the goods that passed along the tracks and sometimes over the ferries.

We noticed before that the main trackways passed close to the flint-mines of Norfolk, Sussex, and Wiltshire, and we can be sure that, in the New Stone Age, the roughed-out axes made near the mines were carried along these tracks to be traded to customers, especially those on Salisbury Plain, to which all of the tracks lead. There must have been well-marked routes over which stone axes were carried from Cumberland and North Wales to Wessex; but the line they took can only be guessed at.

Once bronze became abundant most of the flint-mines would eventually have become idle. But instead, the tin of Cornwall had to be transported along the ridgeways to reach Wessex and northern England. In the Early Bronze Age weapons made of Irish copper and bronze began to arrive in small numbers in western and southern Britain. Gold from south-eastern Ireland also found its way here and to the Continent in the same period. By the Late Bronze Age seven times as many jewels of Irish gold were being exported to Britain as in the Early Bronze Age. At the end of the Age amber from the Baltic was reaching even western Britain. Altogether the trade in bronze, amber, and gold indicates much coming and going of shipping round our coasts.

With the coming of iron-using peoples there is some evidence that the ores of the Forest of Dean and of the Weald of Sussex began to be mined. It was in this period, too, that the tin of Cornwall was exported, especially by sea, in greater quantities than ever before. It was shipped to the mouth of the river Loire in south-western France and then overland to Marseilles, from where it could be shipped again to anywhere in the Mediterranean.

Things to be seen in the Open Air

The ridgeways mentioned in this chapter provide excellent routes for walking tours, and most of them are marked on the Ordnance Survey One-Inch maps. The tracks pass close to many an ancient site and afford constant fine scenery.

In Museums

Hoards of bronze implements. In the Taunton Museum are the remains of the wheel from the lake village.

4: The Coming of the Ploughman: The Late Bronze Age

FROM New Stone Age times until the Late Bronze Age the growing of corn for food had always been less important than the keeping of flocks and herds for meat and milk; and hunting, especially in winter when the cattle were thin and weak and provided poor meat, was a necessary way of keeping up the food supply.

Round about 1000 B.C. bands of refugees arrived on the Sussex coast and founded settlements. They had been forced to leave their homes in northern France by people similar to themselves, who in turn were being pushed westward and southward by German invaders who had crossed the River Elbe in search of new lands for their quickly growing numbers. If you have ever watched an engine shunting wagons you will understand what I mean. The shunting engine, that set the trucks in motion, was the German tribes, and the wagons bumping each other forward were the many Celtic tribes living between the Elbe and the west European coast. At the same time as these refugees were settling in Sussex others, having the same way of life, were arriving in small numbers in eastern England and in Wessex and Cornwall.

Instead of scratching the soil with hoes, these new invaders used a plough drawn by oxen. This meant that a larger area could be cultivated than before, since the plough works faster than the hoe; and it meant also that better crops could be grown because the soil was turned over and aerated more thoroughly. Most of the ancient fields to be seen on the downlands of southern England were probably not formed until at least 500 years later than the time of which we are speaking. We cannot be sure of this because the fields of the Late Bronze Age are very much like those of the Early Iron Age which followed. The later people would have gladly used fields already there and waiting only to be ploughed and sown. To break up grassland for new plots was a heavy and long task, and not to be undertaken if suitable fields were to be had without effort. Usually there is nothing on the surface to show that they had continued in use from the one Age to the other, and only excavation might prove such a continuity; but so far very few field-systems have been investigated.

Yet we do know for certain that there were 'Celtic' fields, as they are called, before the Iron Age. About twenty years ago three barrows were carefully excavated on Marley-combe Hill, Bower Chalke, in the extreme south of Wilt-shire. Pottery found in them showed that they were heaped up over burials of the Late Bronze Age. In making the barrows the mourners had covered a bank which had been formed earlier on one side of a 'Celtic' field. Clearly, then, the field was older than the barrows. And additional proof can be given. On Milston Down, in the parish of Shipton Bellinger, Wiltshire, may be seen a long ditch running across a hillside. Ditches of this particular kind (and we shall hear more about their purpose and shape) have been excavated in several parts of Wessex, and most of them probably belong to the Late Bronze Age (map, p. 56, Grim's Ditch). But the ditch on Milston Down cuts through and across a whole number of 'Celtic' fields, and is obviously later in date of construc-tion. Similar fields cover many thousands of acres in many parts of England, but it is not likely that many of them can ever be proved to be older than the Early Iron Age. Those that I have just mentioned are therefore of special interest.

1a. Pimperne long barrow, Dorset. (*Ashmolean Museum*)

1b. An aerial photograph of henge monuments, cursus, barrows, pits, and Iron Age ditches at Dorchester, Oxon.
(*Ashmolean Museum*)

2a. Burial chamber of long barrow. Wayland's Smithy of the Cotswold type, Ashbury, Berks.

2b. Burial chamber of long barrow. Kit's Coty of the Medway type, near Aylesford, Kent.

3a. A bowl barrow, Oakley Down, Dorset.

3b. A Bronze Age burial cist, Grimslake, Dartmoor.

4a. Avebury henge monument. Sarsens, bank, and ditch.

4b. Sarsens at Avebury henge monument.

5. Stonehenge trilithons, showing tenon joint on hindmost upright stone.

6a. Grimspound: hut-circle with doorway in foreground and the outer pound wall behind.

6b. Late Bronze Age ranch boundary: Grim's Ditch on Blagdon Hill, Cranborne Chase.

7a. An Early Iron Age farmstead and pound (centre) and associated field boundary of stones (foreground), 'Round Pound', Kestor, Dartmoor.

7b. Ditch and banks of an Early Iron Age plateau fort, Cholesbury, Bucks.

8. An Early Iron Age hill-fort, Barbury Castle, near Swindon.

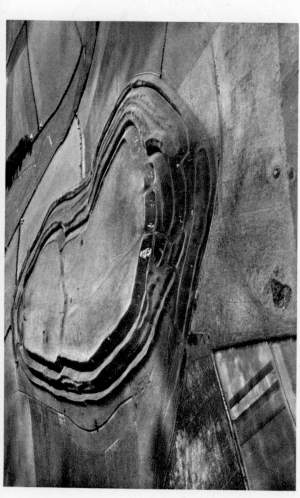

9. An Early Iron Age hill-fort, Maiden Castle, near Dorchester, Dorset. Note the barrows, foreground, right. (*Aerofilms*)

10. A Belgic shield from the Thames at Battersea, of bronze with red glass studs each made of four pieces held together by a bronze swastika. *c.* 50 B.C.–A.D. 20. (*British Museum*)

11a. Verulamium. The south wall of the Roman town.

11b. Verulamium. The Roman theatre.

12a. A Roman road as a terrace-way, Morgan's Hill, near Devizes, Wilts.

12b. Probable Romano-British barrows beside a Roman road at Badbury, Dorset.

13a. The Wansdyke, at Morgan's Hill.

13b. Bokerly Ditch on Blagdon Hill, Hants, with Cranborne
Chase in the background.

14. A Roman fort of the Saxon Shore: Burgh Castle, Suffolk. A fallen bastion is seen left of centre.

15. Grim's Ditch, Berkhamsted Common, Herts.

16a. An Early Iron Age fort which became a mediaeval castle and city – Old Sarum, Wilts. (*Anthony Clark*)

16b. Shadow-site of Celtic fields (background) with what is possibly a Saxon moot-site (foreground) at Chute Causeway, Wilts. (*Anthony Clark*)

Of all prehistoric earthworks, 'Celtic' fields are by far the most common (see overleaf). So many exist in some regions that only a few can be shown on the one-inch map. I remember some years ago walking from Maiden Newton in Dorset along a little valley through the hamlets of Wynford Eagle and Compton Abbas to the great Iron Age fort of Eggardon. It was in several ways a delightful and curious experience. We felt as though the time machine had taken us back a hundred years as we wandered along the lane, opening and closing gates from time to time, and never seeing a building or vehicle that could not have been in use when Queen Victoria was a girl. But other sights took us much farther back in time. For almost the whole distance of five miles the hillsides seemed to be covered with 'Celtic' fields and what looked like the sites of farmsteads where the cultivators lived. We had the feeling on that late summer afternoon that we were discoverers, for very few of these fields were marked on the map. But a year or two after, the whole region was photographed from the air, and detailed maps were produced of all its earthworks. When these have been carefully studied and the results published, we should know much more about ancient farming.

Not many of us have the opportunity of seeing groups of Celtic fields from the air; but if we are in the right regions we can easily see them from the ground. The best time to look for them is soon after sunrise or within an hour or two of sunset. With the sun low, the banks that usually occur on two sides of each field throw a shadow, and it is the shadows which make clear the shapes of the fields and their relationship to the old tracks leading to them, and possibly to the farmstead site, if one is present. (Figure A overleaf is a shadow site seen from the air.)

The fields are roughly square, oblong, or of the shape of a broad diamond, and compared with modern fields, quite

D

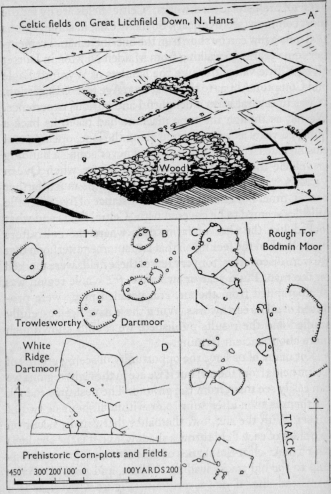

Celtic fields on Great Litchfield Down, N. Hants

Wood

B

Trowlesworthy Dartmoor

C Rough Tor
Bodmin Moor

White
Ridge
Dartmoor

D

Prehistoric Corn-plots and Fields

450' 300'200'100' 0 100 YARDS 200

TRACK

Prehistoric Fields and Corn-plots: (A) Celtic fields and fieldways, Great Litchfield Down, near Burghclere, Hants; (B) Hut-circles and pounds enclosing corn-plots, Trowlesworthy, Dartmoor; (C) Field-lynchets, huts, and enclosures, Rough Tor, Bodmin Moor; (D) Hut-circles and fields, White Ridge, Dartmoor small (see opposite). A plot of four acres is about the largest size that you are likely to see, and they may be of only half that area. Opposite sides of a field are seldom parallel and they are seldom curved. The shape of each plot is dependent on the slope of the ground.

The banks, or lynchets as they are called, are hardly noticeable when you walk over them, except on a steep slope which has not been ploughed in later times. These lynchets were formed by ancient cultivation. When the ground was first broken for ploughing, the turf was stripped off and then the soil was turned by the plough. As the field was on a slope the earth would tend to move a little downhill with each ploughing. What is more, both wind and rain would constantly move crumbs of soil down the slope, so that after hundreds of years the upper part of the field would have a very thin layer of top-soil, and at the lower end movement of earth would be checked by the low wall of turf taken originally from the surface. Very slowly the shifting earth piled up against the bottom bank to form a positive lynchet. But at the upper end of the field the soil had slowly slipped away down the slope, leaving a low bank of untouched earth to mark the point where ploughing began. This bank is a negative lynchet. Where one field touches another on a slope, a positive would form immediately above a negative one, giving the appearance of a much higher bank than where a positive lynchet occurs alone. Field boundaries running up and down a slope are hardly affected. It is those running across a slope which show up most.

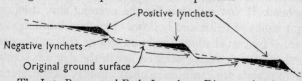

The Late Bronze and Early Iron Ages. Diagram showing formation of lynchets

The ancient lanes leading to the fields usually appear as long narrow strips of unploughed turf running between the lynchets. If a lane runs across the slope there will be a positive lynchet all along the upper side of the lane and a negative along its lower side. If it shows at all, the farmstead will be seen as a roughly circular or oval patch of vegetation: sometimes as a neatly shaped oval of gorse or nettles; sometimes as brighter and richer grass.

The building of a farmstead required excavation into the chalk for a foot or two. In this hollow collected much of the household rubbish, which was allowed to pile up on the floor. Once the buildings were deserted (often in the later part of the fourth century A.D.), vegetation re-invaded the spot, and where the hollow foundations had been dug, grass and bushes found a deeper, moister, and richer root run. Consequently, plants can flourish on these sites which could not exist on the shallower soil around. Where, however, the whole is covered with grass and small herbs, they grow more lush, and a sharp eye can tell from the greenness of the turf where there has been a lowering of the chalk undersoil.

This is true also of ancient ditches and of positive lynchets. They also provide a deeper and moister soil on which grass is greener, especially after a spell of dry weather. On the other hand, wherever the top-soil has been thinned out, as for example near a negative lynchet, the grass will become brown much sooner in times of drought. These differences in the colour of the turf, and in the kinds of plants growing, will often show up an ancient site even when the sun is high overhead. If you can wait for the evening sun, then the slight banks of fields and hollows of ancient buildings are revealed by cast shadows, and you will be able to discover whether your detective work earlier in the day was sound. Where rabbits are common in chalk country they prefer to burrow in the looser soil of banks, and the white rubble thrown out from their holes often shows up at a distance in any light and reveals the pattern of the earthworks. As we shall see later, there may be yet further clues to prehistoric occupation.

One of the earliest farmsteads of the Late Bronze Age ploughmen so far discovered is on Plumpton Plain on the South Downs, six miles north of Brighton. It dates from about 950 B.C. Although only faint traces are now to be seen of it among the bushes, the walk up from Falmer to the edge of the escarpment is a pleasant one. Fine views across the Weald present themselves, and by turning left (west-wards) and walking along the green track, you will see a number of barrows and various ditches, and at Ditchling Beacon are the faint traces of an Iron Age fort.

On Plumpton Plain itself four oval enclosures were ex-cavated, each of about 100 feet across, surrounded by a bank which once had strong fences on top. Within each enclosure was a round hut, twenty feet across. From these came pottery that showed the farmers to have come from northern France. The place was not occupied for long, but a new group of farms was built nearby, and the farmers seem to have married local women, judging from the pottery. New refugees with winged axes had also arrived; this time the emigrants were from south Germany. From Plumpton Plain, and from other refugee settlements, we learn that corn was grown and that cattle, sheep, and perhaps horses were kept. They were put out to pasture on the downland slopes that face north, for they get less sun and grow poorer crops than those facing south, which were in fact broken up into small fields.

In Hampshire, Dorset, Berkshire, and Wiltshire the boundary ditches of vast Late Bronze Age cattle pastures can still be clearly seen on the ground (Pl. 6b), and from the air it is possible to understand their purpose. If you can manage to borrow Dr O. G. S. Crawford's book, *Archae-ology in the Field* you will see maps of them on pp. 108–18. In eastern Wiltshire they cover a distance of twelve miles on the downs along both sides of the little river Bourne.

The ditches round two of these cattle ranches near Cholderton remain almost complete. One of them takes in a big oblong of pasture two and a half miles long by a third of a mile wide. Air photographs of Quarley Hill show one of the ditches coming within the defences of the later Iron Age hill-fort. When they are carefully excavated the boundary ditches are found to have been dug in the form of a 'V', but with the bottom flat (see diagram below, and Pl. 6b). The soil and rock that had been dug out were usually thrown up on both sides, making the ditch appear much deeper. On these banks at the sides can be found the holes for the posts of fences which once ran along the tops, closing in the ditch. It is likely that the boundary ditches were used for driving cattle down to the river for water, and back again to the pastures. The flat bottom allowed the animals to plod along in single file, and the steep sides and fences at the top prevented them from straying. One man, or even one well-trained dog, could have managed a large herd without difficulty between the watering-place and even the farther part of the pasture. The map on p. 56 shows one of these ranch-boundaries called 'Grim's Ditch', a name given by the Saxons to earthworks of several kinds and of

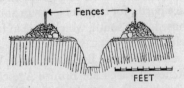

Late Bronze and Early Iron Ages.
Section of a ranch-boundary ditch

different periods. Grim was another name for their god Woden who, they believed, had built these earthworks.

On Boscombe Down, Allington, Wiltshire, there is a cattle enclosure of about a quarter of an acre which uses a boundary ditch for one of its sides. Unlike earthworks of earlier peoples this one has almost straight banks and ditches. Several similar enclosures are known, and it is thought that they served to give winter shelter to the herds that roamed the Late Bronze Age ranches in summer.

The name given to the builders of the boundary ditches is the clumsy one of Deverel-Rimbury, taken from two of their burial sites in Dorset. They came across to Britain from the Dutch and French coasts about 750 B.C., and were probably descendants of the Urnfield and even earlier peoples. The men were armed with swords, spears, and axes, and they defended their bodies with round shields of bronze. Their craftsmen in wood and metal were equipped with a much wider range of tools than ever before, and their farmers, besides having a wooden plough to turn over the soil, could reap their corn with an efficient bronze sickle (see figure D, p. 82).

In the house food could be cooked over the fire in great bronze cauldrons imported from Ireland; but only the richest could afford them, and they were looked upon as a sign of high rank. There were improvements in the method of spinning yarn: an upright loom came into use, and the warp threads of cloth were held taut by clay loom-weights. The spindles, too, were weighted with 'whorls' so that they might turn the faster. The clothes made on these looms were sometimes adorned with ornaments of Irish gold.

The dead were burned on a pyre and their ashes were sometimes put in the side of an older barrow, or, rarely, in smaller and lower barrows made specially for the purpose. Commonly the ashes were put in an urn. The pots of the

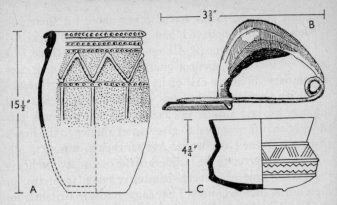

Late Bronze and Early Iron Ages: (A) Deverel-Rimbury urn containing a cremation, Latch Farm urnfield, near Christchurch, Hants; (B) Early Iron Age brooch, Boroughbridge, Yorks; (C) Early Iron Age pot from farmstead at All Cannings Cross, near Devizes, Wilts

Deverel-Rimbury people are of all sizes from seven to seventeen or more inches high, of many shapes, and with a great variety of decorative patterns. In prehistoric times each people (the Beaker Folk, for instance) made pots all having a family likeness; changes in shape and decoration occur only slowly over a long period of time. The variations in the Deverel-Rimbury urns are probably due to the mixed ancestry of those people on the Continent and to their inter-marriage with the earlier inhabitants of southern Britain.

Often they buried their dead without any sign remaining on the surface of the ground, even though there may be as many as a hundred burials in a single urnfield. Not all the cremations were put in urns, but they are clearly burials of people of the same tribe as those that were placed in pots. The large numbers of cremations found together in one place indicate that an urnfield is the cemetery of a large village, much larger than had ever existed before in Britain. The herdsmen and hoe-men of the New Stone Age and

Earlier Bronze Ages could not settle in large groups like this. Their farming methods made frequent removals necessary if they were to continue to win enough food from the soil. Each group of fields could be used for only a few years, and when it was exhausted they had to move on.

In Dorset alone about 600 burials of Deverel-Rimbury people are known, and there must be many more to be found. In the south of England as a whole they are more in number than the burials of all earlier peoples together. They indicate a growth in the size of the population that had been impossible under the old system of farming. But the new system was to last for only about 300 years. Then iron-using tribes began to swarm into England and overcome the older people in the way that has happened so often in our pre-history and history.

Things to be seen in the Open Air

Barrows, especially in the New Forest, and Celtic fields, though few are actually of the late Bronze Age. Boundary ditches of cattle-ranches of which the following are a few good examples: Grim's Ditch (though recently much destroyed by ploughing) on the northern edge of Cranborne Chase, Dorset; on both sides of the river Bourne, Wiltshire; Baydon, Wiltshire; near Lambourn and between Wantage and Streatley, Berkshire; short stretches in Hampshire and Dorset; others on the Wolds of the East Riding of Yorkshire. Farms, fields, and tracks on Plumpton Plain (see p. 101), Park Brow, near Worthing and Harrow Hill, Patching – all in Sussex.

In Museums

Chiefly urns and bronze implements.

5: The Coming of Iron

WE have seen already that some of the Late Bronze Age invaders knew the use of iron, but they must have obtained their tools from the Continent; almost certainly there was no mining and smelting of ore in Britain until after the arrival of people who could recognize iron ore and produce from it weapons and tools. The first of the new series of invasions began between 450 and 400 B.C. when new people made settlements in southern and eastern England from Devon to Yorkshire. In time they penetrated to the Bristol Channel and to the region round Oxford, though a few settlements were made even beyond the river Severn. A line drawn from Exeter to Whitby in Yorkshire roughly suggests the northern limits of the Iron Age 'A' culture, as it is called (see map on p. 117).

The bronze implements and burial urns of the Deverel-Rimbury tribes soon ceased to be made; and just as these people had enslaved the Urn people and Wessex warriors, so they, in their turn, now became slaves labouring on the fields for the new settlers. No doubt in many places they were forced to work on the very land that their forefathers had brought into cultivation and which they themselves had owned. This must have happened again and again in prehistory, and later the Romans did much the same thing to the Britons. The Saxons also reduced many of these people to slavery, and the Normans in their turn dispossessed the Anglo-Saxons as overlords. Time after time warlike invaders, hungry for land, sailed from the Continent to the harbours of our east and south coasts. Seldom large in number, they were, however, usually stronger in weapons and fighting power; and they conquered and subdued the older races that had taken the land before them.

But again and again the tide of conquest that swept across lowland Britain stopped short of the highland zone as is shown on the map on p. 86. This zone, to the north and west of a line joining the two great river estuaries of Severn and Humber, was poorer in all respects. Its soils and climate do not favour farming, and so invaders did not think it worth while to conquer. In any case, with its mountains and passes it was easier to defend than the lowlands, and even the gold and tin to be found in the highland zone did not attract the big and well-organized attack which would have been necessary to subdue it. In fact, before the Middle Ages only the Romans had sufficient strength to conquer Wales, and even they failed in Scotland.

But though there was no easy road for the conqueror into the mountains and moors of the West and North, refugees fleeing from the invaders of lowland Britain found a safe resting-place in the highland zone. Almost throughout prehistory it was a haven for those who had been forced to flee from the fat lands of the South and East; and most of us remember that the Britons fled westward before the invading Saxons and continued to resist them for long after the earliest English settlers had come.

So it was with the Iron Age conquerors; lowland Britain became theirs. With their iron swords and spears they outmatched the Bronze Age tribes in battle; and with their cheap iron tools, which they could easily replace when broken or worn, they could without difficulty fell trees to make new fields, which their iron plough-shares could turn with a stronger furrow. Like the farmers of all ages before them, they hunted in the vast forests, and kept herds of cattle and sheep. But far more than any earlier people they sent their ox-ploughs up onto the chalk downlands and carved out more and more fields (see p. 98). Even the cattle pastures of the Late Bronze Age were often ploughed up. And now, in addition to the older wheat and barley, they began to grow oats, rye, and beans; and because the climate had become damper, the harvested corn, except that to be used for the following year's sowing, had to be dried in ovens. Without drying, the bread corn would have sprouted or become infected with mildew.

A farm of this period was discovered from the air in 1924 and was so brilliantly excavated in 1938–9 (see p. 111) that it is possible to reconstruct it with a great deal of certainty. It was situated a mile south of the place that was to become Salisbury, and beside the ridgeway which comes up from the ancient ford at Britford. The ridgeway runs westward for eighteen miles along the chalk downs without crossing a single brook. Let us mount the time machine on the west bank of the river Avon and travel back to about 250 years before Christ was born and 2,200 years from now.

*

The river is low this year, for the summer has been less wet than it usually is. Crossing the ford comes a man with a large skin bag over his shoulder, and he bends under its weight. He sees us and hails us, asking us to wait for him. Wearily he drags his refreshed feet from the shallow water and approaches with a smile. As he speaks a crane flaps slowly overhead and utters his loud trumpet blast, and a kingfisher flashes like a blue dart between the alders and willows of the marshy flats beside the river.

With strange speech the pedlar, for such he is, asks us to buy from his stock of fine pots, made with the finest clay and baked to the hardness of flint, and burnished till they shine like red bronze. As he praises his wares he forgets his

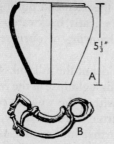

The Early Iron Age:
(A) Iron Age 'C' bead-rim urn, Jordan's Hill, Weymouth;
(B) Brooch, the Danes' Graves, near Great Driffield, Yorks

weariness, and smiles with forced pleasantness as he withdraws a pot from his bag. He offers them cheap, he says, for not one has he sold in a day's march. Pots are not as often broken as they used to be and business is bad.

As he sees that we will not buy, his manner changes to his old tiredness, and, shouldering his pack, he begins the long uphill walk to the farm. Just above the alder-thicket we come to rough grass-land with our track several feet deep going straight up and through a gate in a fence. Near the gate stands a group of small and shaggy cattle which, after a moment of staring doubt, stampede away from the strangers with snorts and thundering hooves.

Beyond the gate we find ourselves following the track between small fields, each one with a negative lynchet at the top of the slope and a positive at the bottom, like broad irregular steps or terraces ascending the hill (see p. 99). On one side stands the tall stubble of barley, for only the ears are reaped with the iron sickles. On the other side a plough is being dragged through knee-deep weeds by slow plodding oxen. In turn the ploughman prods them with his goad then stares in fear towards these unknown men, who may be the vanguard of a host of raiders for all he knows. Then he recognizes the potter, waves his goad in greeting, and turns his eyes back to the furrow. All the while the ploughboy has been chanting sweetly to the oxen and pulling hard on their wooden yoke as he steps neatly backwards down the field. We pass without his knowing of our presence, so faithful is he to his task.

As we climb farther, a shoulder of the hill sinks below our line of sight and we catch our first glimpse of the farm. Dogs are yapping excitedly from within the wooden palisade; a flock of great bustards a quarter of a mile away, but conspicuous on the crest of a farther hill, scuttle off with all speed into the distance. The slamming of the two heavy farm gates at our approach seems to have startled the whole countryside, man, beast, and bird.

Coming nearer to the great palisade of split logs, pointed on top, we notice scavenger kites quarrelling among the garbage in the ditch outside; and a raven busily tearing the flesh from the head of a wolf nailed to the fence as a warning to his fellows. These great birds are too busy with their feasting to notice the commotion all around. More warily, buzzards glide in wide circles high overhead waiting for silence before they again descend to hunt for the small animals that abound near a farm.

On our near approach to the gates they are opened, for we are now recognized as peaceful travellers. We are welcomed in with hospitable looks, and bidden to sit down while the water is brought to lave our feet. This allows us a few moments to study our surroundings. The outer palisade is in the form of a rough circle over a hundred yards across. Its double gates swing on a central post and the openings on each side of it are too narrow to allow the entrance of a wagon. In the centre of the courtyard is a spacious circular house with a roof of green turves rising towards the centre in a flat cone. Smoke is coming from an opening at the very top of the roof. A rough path from the outer gateway leads direct to a timber porch which shelters the house-door.

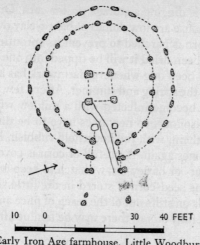

Early Iron Age farmhouse, Little Woodbury,
near Salisbury, Wilts

On the south side of the house are a number of upright posts with sagging lines strung between them, on which are hung many bundles of ears of corn drying in the sun. At the first threat of rain the hide ropes can be untied, and the precious seed corn for next year's crop can be quickly carried to the shelter of open sheds. On one of the posts hangs the furry hide of a great brown bear from which every morsel of fat has been carefully removed with flint scrapers. Beyond are low fences surrounding six or seven large holes in the ground. From one of them juts a ladder made from a single timber upright with crosspieces a foot apart for rungs. A man comes up into sight, white with chalk-dust and bearing on his shoulder a large wicker basket. He tips the chalk rubble from it into a similar pit near by and then disappears again into the hole from which he has just emerged. Then a woman appears from the rear of the house and shoots some household rubbish into the pit where the chalk has been thrown.

The man is digging a storage pit for corn. On the other side of the house are low domes of baked-clay ovens where the bread corn is parched to prevent its sprouting in store. After it has been dried it will be tipped into one of the new pits that has been dug whenever farmwork has allowed the time during the spring and summer. After a few years these storage-pits become infected with a mildew which makes the corn poisonous, so new ones have to be dug, and the chalk from them, with the household rubbish, helps to fill up the old ones again. A pit full of corn is covered with a roof of wheat- or barley-straw thatch to keep out the rain. The precious seed-corn is stored in the little square shed which stands on stilts out of the reach of mice and damp. If it is not carefully stored there may be famine after the next harvest.

Soon the water for our feet is brought, and clear fresh water to drink. Then we are led inside the house to eat. Within the outer door we find ourselves in gloom, for there are no windows. But we can see that an alleyway about seven feet wide leads off on each side between the outer wall and an inner one. This is built of thinner timbers between which clay has been rammed to keep out draughts. During winter nights this circular alleyway provides warm covered shelter for the plough oxen and the few breeding cattle that can be spared from the autumn slaughter. The small hardy sheep can find enough bite on the chalk pastures and the corn stubbles, and the swine can rout about for roots and beech-mast and acorns in the riverside woods. Only a very little corn can be spared for the cattle to keep them alive through the dark hungry months of winter.

The main circular room has no furniture apart from some broad shelves which serve as beds by night and benches by day. On one of them lies a coverlet made of the skins of many wild cats sewn together. On another is a fine fur of bear, similar to the one being cured out in the sun. And there is a third made up of hundreds of skins of the red squirrel.

In the middle of the room an open square of four great tree-trunks supports the heavy turf roof. In spite of the large hole left in its centre the room seems full of bitter smoke, which makes our eyes smart and weep. Tired with all the strangeness of a distant age and its ways of living, we sink down on to the bench, and, ignoring the food brought to us, we fall asleep.

*

Besides Little Woodbury, as the spot is now called, a number of other farmsteads or hamlets of the Early Iron Age have been excavated, although none has yielded such a clear picture of how people lived at that time. Most of these other sites are on the downs of Wiltshire, and the best known are All Cannings Cross, in the Vale of Pewsey, and Swallowcliffe Down and Fifield Bavant Down in south Wiltshire. From the style of the pottery it has been estimated that these places were inhabited from about 400 to 300 B.C.

Each of them had from eighty to a hundred pits in use at different times for the storage of wheat, barley, and oats. Some of the pits were covered with boughs of birch and hazel, meeting at the centre (like the ribs of an open umbrella) and bound together there. This framework was daubed with a mixture of clay and chalk and then thatched with straw to keep out the rain. Sometimes this roofing caught fire and baked the daub, with the marks of thatch preserved on one side and of the boughs on the other. The collapsed remnants in the pit make it possible to say how the roofs were built. In some pits burnt grains of the three kinds of corn were found.

The hamlet at All Cannings Cross was probably surrounded by a stockade like the one at Woodbury, but inside it there were several huts placed here and there without planning. These houses were not round but rectangular in shape and they were thatched. Because of the danger of fire, cooking was done in the open air. For roasting meat a hole was dug and packed round with hot stones. The meat was put inside and more hot stones were added on top. The oven was then covered with turf to keep in the heat for as long as possible. Even so, the meat would have been too underdone for our liking.

Sheep, cattle, pigs, goats, and horses were kept for food, and dogs added to the liveliness of the farmyard. Meat supplies were increased by hunting deer; and birds, too, were occasionally snared for the pot.

While the men worked in the little square fields near the

$7\frac{3}{4}''$

villages, the women ground corn for bread, cooked, span yarn and wove it into cloth, and made the household pots which they decorated by pressing their fingertips into the clay before they dried it. The potter's wheel was unknown as yet, and pots were made by building up clay rings from a flat base. A male occupation was the smelting of iron and some

Early Iron Age pot from farmstead at Park Brow, near Worthing, Sussex

working in bronze. The iron could have been obtained from near Heddington, a few miles to the west.

In the last few years a farmstead of this period has been excavated at Kestor (Castor on the map), near Chagford on Dartmoor. The house was in many ways similar to the one at Little Woodbury, circular and with inner timber posts to support the heavy turf roof; but the outer wall, still well preserved (Pl. 7a), is of stone. Round about are many fields with stone walls clearly visible and a hand-mill from the house shows that corn was grown. In a working-place an iron-smelting furnace with slag was found, the first certain evidence of iron-using people from Dartmoor. The discovery of a spindle-whorl reveals that cloth was woven. Pottery from the house showed that it was occupied from some time after 400 B.C. by Iron Age 'A' people, and there were indications that they had lived there for a long time. Similar houses, but of the later Iron Age 'B' people, have been found in Cornwall in the promontory fort at Trevelgue (near Newquay) at Castle Dor (near Fowey) and St Mawgan (near Newquay).

Things to be seen in the Open Air

The sites of these farms and hamlets have little to show.

In Museums

Most of the objects from the sites already mentioned in this chapter may be seen in the Devizes and Salisbury Museums.

Hill-forts

As we have seen, the Iron Age settlers were in some ways similar to the Late Bronze Age tribes whom they displaced, especially in the size and shape of their fields and sometimes in the shape of their houses. No doubt the new and the old peoples gradually merged, though some of the bronze-users were perhaps pushed westward, as had happened to conquered people of the lowlands before this time and as was to happen again.

But the Iron Age people brought with them several customs that were new to Britain. For example, they very seldom buried their dead with care and ceremony; in fact, few of their burials have ever been found. Many thousands of Bronze Age burials are known, but very few of their dwellings; Iron Age dwelling-sites, on the other hand, have provided most of the material which enables us to reconstruct their way of life but their burials tell us little except that they had no fixed custom. Some of their dead have been found cremated and some unburned, but parts of human skeletons have often come to light in rubbish pits, and in a few instances the bones had been fashioned into objects of use: a cup made from part of a skull, a scoop from an arm-bone, and a spindle-whorl from a knee-cap. Sometimes corpses were thrown carelessly into a pit with old rubbish; in others only broken fragments of a skeleton were found. Does this suggest head-hunting and cannibal-feasts? If so, it would not be the only evidence from prehistory. We have clear proof from New Stone Age times that human bones were cracked open to get at the marrow inside. But we must beware of jumping to conclusions. These human remains may be those of slaves or criminals that had been thrown to the dogs after death. We cannot be sure.

But one new Iron Age custom has left a strong mark on the face of modern England, and in our travels through the countryside we must be very unobservant if we have not noticed one or two hill-forts crowning a stretch of downland. In Wiltshire, Dorset, Hampshire, and Sussex many of these forts are to be seen, and no southern county, and indeed few throughout Britain, are altogether without them (Pls. 7b, 8 and 9. Almost all of those known in England and Wales are shown in the map opposite.)

Although New Stone Age herdsmen made camps where, in summer, at any rate, they lived, and sheltered their cattle,

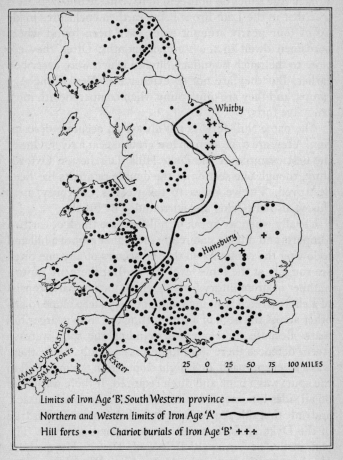

Map showing the limits of Early Iron Age 'A' and 'B' and the distribution of hill-forts and chariot burials

Bronze Age tribes do not seem to have made hill-forts. It is true that in the Late Bronze Age earthen enclosures made up of four nearly straight sides have been found where herdsmen dwelt in the summer months. Often they are close to the ranch boundary-ditches which were described earlier. But they are not so extensive as New Stone Age camps, and they are quite puny when compared with most Iron Age forts.

The name 'hill-fort' is not always an accurate description. A few are to be seen on low ground near a river. One of the best examples is the Dyke Hills, Dorchester, Oxfordshire, though one section of the double ramparts has been destroyed. Twelve miles to the west is Cherbury, near Pusey, also low-lying and surrounded by brooks.

Usually when we speak of hill-forts we think of earthen ramparts and ditches encircling the higher part of a hill and following the contours, so that all sectors of any one ditch are roughly at the same level (Pl. 8). But there are quite a number of promontory forts in which the ramparts consist of a short stretch running from one very steep slope to another across the neck of a spur jutting out from a larger hill mass. Because the slopes surrounding the spur were so steep, defences there were unnecessary. Only where there was a level approach, or a slight slope, from the main hill to the spur, was a bank and ditch required. If there was water on all sides but one, only that side was open to easy attack, and only that side required earthwork defences. This is true of the Dyke Hills, Dorchester, mentioned just now. The cliff castles of Cornwall; Bolt Tail, Devon; Hengistbury Head near Christchurch, Hampshire; Worlebury, near Weston-super-Mare, Somerset; St David's Head, Pembrokeshire; Castle Ditches, near Llantwit Major, Glamorgan; Combs Moss, Chapel-en-le-Frith, Derby; and probably the Danes Dykes, Flamborough Head, Yorkshire, are widely scattered examples of promontory forts, one of which is within reach of most people either at home or on holiday.

Inland, where the steepness of the hillsides served the same defensive purpose as cliffs and sea, there are many promontory forts, some quite small like the one called the Giant's Grave on the north side of the Vale of Pewsey, Wiltshire. More impressive examples may be seen on Butser Hill, near Petersfield, Hampshire; at Leckhampton near Cheltenham; in Lydney Park, Forest of Dean; and Boltby Scar, near Thirsk, Yorkshire. There are many other lesser ones, some waiting to be discovered. Where the lie of the land made a complete ring of entrenchments unnecessary, a vast amount of heavy manual labour was avoided.

The enormous task of building an Early Iron Age fort is well illustrated by Cissbury, near Worthing, Sussex. True, it is probably the largest camp made by the first of the three waves of Iron Age invaders; yet a camp of half the area would involve much more than half the labour that went to the making of Cissbury.

It covers about sixty acres, and is on the same site as a number of New Stone Age flint mines, which can be seen in the western end of the camp. The single bank and ditch of

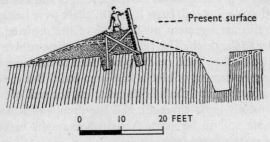

The Early Iron Age: the rampart of Hollingbury
hill-fort, Brighton

the fort cover another eighteen acres. To construct them 35,000 cubic yards of solid chalk had to be dug with antler picks from the ditch and carried in wicker-baskets to be piled systematically to form the rampart. This was faced with timber to prevent the loose chalk from rolling forward and down from the bank into the ditch. The facing (called properly a revetment) was carried above the top of the bank, rather like the battlements of a castle, to provide protection against the missiles of an attacker. But the timber for revetting was obtained by felling and shaping 8,000 to 12,000 uprights fifteen feet high.

Either this vast undertaking took a long time or there were very many willing hands to help. If, however, it had taken a long time, the danger that was threatening (a new invasion by another group of Iron Age tribes) might have passed, and the work might then have been left unfinished. This actually happened to a similar fort, Ladle Hill, six miles from Newbury in Berkshire; and it is possible to learn from it how such a fort was made.

First the line of the ditch was marked out with a plough furrow. Gangs of men (and women, too, no doubt) were then given sections of ditch to dig, each gang working along until it joined the next. There was no woodland close enough, or the danger was too imminent, to allow of timber revetting, so, instead, large lumps of chalk were heaped up in careful arrangement on the side of the growing bank nearest to the ditch. The turf and small chalk rubble were dumped farther back, ready to be added to the bank when a strong revetment of blocks had been built. But the work got no further, and the half-dug ditches, the wall of blocks (now mostly grass-covered), and the dumps of loose material are still to be seen. Aerial photographs make the whole matter very clear.

About three dozen of these earliest Iron Age hill-forts are

known. They are to be seen in an area of southern and eastern England bounded by a line running from south Devon to Yorkshire. Within this region many other things besides forts have been found to prove the presence of the Iron Age 'A' people, as they are called.

Most of these forts were built because of the threat of new invasions by other Iron Age tribes from the Marne region in north-eastern France. The very first Iron Age tribes began to settle here from about five centuries before Christ, but danger did not seriously threaten them for another 300 years (about 250 to 200 B.C.). They then strengthened the few hill-forts already built and began to construct others such as Ladle Hill. But the danger subsided and some of the forts were abandoned. Others gave shelter to a small permanent population of farmers, whose numbers were increased in time of danger by the people from a wide area around. The size of the forts made it possible for these outsiders to drive their flocks and herds before them into the shelter of the ramparts. These are simple, with only one ditch and bank, and with plain entrances, mere gaps in the banks closed only

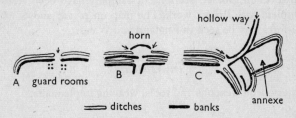

The development of hill-fort entrances: (A) simple; (B) horned (Ffridd Faldwyn, Montgom.); (C) with barbican and annexe (Almondbury, Yorks)

by a wooden gate, and quite easy to attack and storm. Later hill-forts, as we shall see, were altogether more complicated.

Bronze remained for long after 500 B.C. as much in use as

iron, and even flint still had its uses. The blacksmiths now forged narrow ploughshares, bill-hooks, and sickles as their contribution to greatly expanded farming activities. Weaving in finer textures and the use of safety pins instead of buttons for fastening the clothes suggests a little more comfort. And the luxury of salt was probably easier to come by. The 'Red Hills' of the Essex and Lincolnshire coasts and the edge of the Fens are relics of a salt-making industry which seems to have begun at this period.

Most important of all, however, was the great expansion of downland fields brought into cultivation by the first users of iron. Their fields and their farming methods continued in use for almost a thousand years, until the coming of the English.

Things to be seen in the Open Air

Most of the best examples of promontory forts have been mentioned in the chapter. Hill-forts exist in almost every region of Britain, and at Hollingbury, near Brighton, Sussex, and at Lulworth in Dorset, sections of rampart have been restored complete with timber work. The map on p. 117 shows where hill-forts may be seen in England and Wales.

In Museums

Pottery, iron weapons and tools, weaving implements.

The Charioteers and the Lake Dwellers

From about 2000 until about 700 B.C. summer in Britain had been drier and warmer than in the preceding 3,500 years. Gradually, from the seventh century before Christ, the climate changed to a long period of wetter and cooler summers which made the harvesting of corn far more difficult than before. We noticed at Little Woodbury that special arrangements were necessary for drying the grain before it was stored, and that furnaces were in use.

But these problems would not have worried the charioteers from the Marne district of north-eastern France, who invaded and settled in east Yorkshire in about 250 B.C. They were warrior chiefs like the Beaker and Wessex people, and depended on their conquered subjects for bread. Only when the harvest was so bad that they, together with their subjects, suffered actual famine, would these overlords have regretted the constant rain. And they, in any case, would have been the last to go hungry.

This band of Iron Age 'B' invaders is particularly interesting because we know that their tribal name was 'Parisii' and that, later, the larger section of the tribe that stayed in France gave its name to the island which still forms the heart of old Paris. Julius Caesar knew this citadel as Lutetia Parisiorum, and he knew the Parisii through campaigning against them in Gaul. The Greek geographer Ptolemy, who lived in the first half of the second century A.D. actually speaks of a Celtic tribe called the Parisii who were occupying what we know as east Yorkshire. But their burials have been found elsewhere in England; in Cambridgeshire, Lincolnshire, and Suffolk, though only in small numbers (see map on p. 117). Hunsbury, near

Pot from Iron Age 'A' hillfort, the Caburn, Lewes, Sussex, showing the influence of Iron Age 'B' decoration

Northampton, has yielded some of their distinctive goods, and traces of them have been found in Wiltshire, Kent, and Sussex, including Cissbury and the Caburn (Lewes). It seems that here and there Marnian chieftains with a small band of warriors carved out a small territory for themselves and ruled the older Iron Age 'A' tribes.

The most important remains of the Parisii in Yorkshire are the mounds which they raised in some numbers over their dead. Many hundreds of them have been excavated, especially at Arras, near Market Weighton, and also four miles north of Driffield, where the mounds are known as the Danes' Graves (marked 4 on the map on p. 86). Out of a total of 500 of the latter, 200 still survive. Most of them covered the bodies of ordinary people, unburned and in a crouching position, with a few simple ornaments. But one of the larger graves contained the iron tyres, lynch-pins, and other fittings of a chariot that had long ago been the proud possession of one of the two men whose skeletons were discovered with it. Horse-bits had been placed in the grave, but perhaps the horses were too valuable to sacrifice, for there was no trace of them. However, in the year 1812, the skeleton of a warrior, with his long iron sword and golden ornaments, was found between the skeletons of two horses at Mildenhall in north-west Suffolk, so horses were sometimes slaughtered for burial beside their master; and it may be that one of the human skeletons found with the Driffield chariot was that of a driver sacrificed at his lord's burial.

These warriors fought with iron daggers, broadswords, and wooden shields; and their smiths brought metalcraft to a high pitch of excellence, especially in the designs used in decoration. The shield and scabbard-mount found in the river Witham near Lincoln are only two of the beautiful examples of metalcraft made by the Marnians. There are other equally fine products of their smiths to be seen in our museums.

Fighting from two-wheeled chariots seems to have been customary in the east and south-east of Britain. Great skill in driving and in manoeuvring was acquired by Celtic warriors. They could dart out onto the chariot-pole between the two horses and wield their swords standing on the yoke that joined the horses' necks. Even Julius Caesar's highly disciplined troops were at first thrown into confusion when attacked by the Belgic charioteers during his British campaigns of 55 and 54 B.C. The effect of these tactics on the older Iron Age tribes of Britain must have made victory easy for the Marnian, and, later, for the Belgic invaders of this island.

For at least three centuries before the birth of Christ the tin of Cornwall had attracted Greek traders. They carried the metal from a trading centre on St Michael's Mount, across the English Channel at its widest and round the Breton peninsula to the mouth of the river Loire. From there it was carried overland on beasts of burden along a route which took thirty days on foot, to the ports of Marseilles and Narbonne on the Mediterranean Sea.

Iron Age 'B' tribes who had moved south-westwards across France to the ore-bearing regions of northern Spain and Brittany began crossing the Channel to Cornwall some time after 200 B.C. and landed in scattered bands in a countryside occupied by Deverel-Rimbury people (see Chapter 4). It seems that they had come in search of tin-ore and, in fact, one of their brooches has been found in a mine-working near St Austell.

To make their position safe among a hostile population who were now deprived of a very profitable industry, they built promontory forts and round stone forts in dry-walling (that is, without using mortar). The best known of these is Chun Castle near Pendeen, which has an inner wall fifteen feet thick, of large granite blocks, enclosing a circular court-yard about 165 feet across. Outside the wall were two shallow ditches with an outer bank between them. Ranged round the courtyard are eleven oval huts, one of which was a smithy where iron and tin ores were smelted in a furnace. Set on a hill dominating the surrounding countryside, the massive defences of Chun were planned to reduce the risk of surprise attack, for other invaders from over the sea might well come in search of Cornish tin. If they reached the Castle gateway, however, they had an unpleasant surprise, for they had to turn left as they advanced and so exposed their right to attack at close quarters from within the Castle; and the right side was not covered by the shield, since that would have impeded the use of the sword which was carried in the right hand. Peaceful visitors from Portugal, Spain, and Brittany, homelands of these people of Chun, left scraps of their pottery in the huts. Even a sherd from the faraway Mediterranean was discovered.

Chun is not by any means the largest of Cornish forts. There are several larger worth a visit, including the promontory forts to be found above the sea on many Cornish cliffs. The Iron Age villages of the region should not be missed either. We know most about one called Chysauster, three miles to the north of Penzance. Standing guard over it is the fort Castle-an-Dinas, which has three circular ramparts of stone with ditches in between. (There is another, similar, fort of the same name and date two miles east of St Columb Major.)

Chysauster village was occupied from the second century B.C. until late in the Roman period, for nearly 500 years altogether; and in that time many changes were made in the buildings. Sites of eight houses along an irregular street can still be recognized, and no two are quite the same in plan. Yet each has a central courtyard with several rounded rooms opening from it, and one longer one, probably the stable for the ox which helped plough the fields still to be seen round the village. The smaller rooms were dwelling-places, and in some can be seen the hollowed stone which held an upright post supporting the roof of timber and turf. The walls, in places still above shoulder height, are of dry-stone walling with earth and rubble cores. Shallow channels covered with slabs of stone served as drains, or, in one case, as a conduit to bring water to the main room of a house.

Not far to the south of the village was an underground chamber where the inhabitants could hide if, let us suppose, attackers surprised them under cover of a sea-mist and there was no time to reach Castle-an-Dinas. A number of these *fougous*, as they are called in Cornwall, have been discovered. In Carn Euny (Sancreed), one of the many other Iron Age villages of the region, a passage led from inside a house down to a fougou. The entrances of one or two have been found opening into the ditch of a fort. It is likely that their normal use was for the storage of grain, but they would have afforded excellent hiding-places in time of great danger.

In the Land's End district alone at least twenty-three of these undefended villages are known. Their inhabitants' main occupation was farming the Celtic fields, of which the lynchets can still be traced round some of them. Usually six to eight households is the largest number in a village, and these must have been subject to the lord of the nearest castle, whose wealth and power came from the tin which found eager buyers from overseas. Labour in the tin mines may have been provided by slaves, though it is equally possible that the villagers had to spend part of the working year winning ore from the earth.

A visitor to west Cornwall will see at least several great burial chambers like Lanyon Quoit or Chun Quoit. These are the remains of Late Bronze Age round barrows that have lost their earth covering. In the use of the enormous stones they show a close relationship with New Stone Age methods of tomb-building. The Chapel Euny Barrow, near Brane, is another interesting example that still retains some of its earthen covering. But the burial places of those who lived in the lordly Iron Age castles and the humble villages are hardly known. At Harlyn Bay, two and a half miles due west of Padstow, about 140 burials of the third century B.C. (and later) were found as skeletons doubled up in stone cists like Beaker Folk. With the burials were brooches, pins, and broken pottery, some of which seemed to indicate that these small men and women, of under five feet five inches in height, had come from southern France or northern Spain after a fairly long stay in Brittany. In the museum nearby some of the burials may be seen just as they were discovered in the sand, enclosed within stone slabs.

It was not only Cornwall that proved attractive to these Iron Age 'B' tribes from across the Channel; other bands settled in Devon, Somerset, and Dorset, and gradually they penetrated to South Devon and Dorset by sea and along the Bristol Channel to south Wales and the Cotswolds (map, p. 117), and, most important from their point of view, to the Forest of Dean, where iron ore was to be found, and where vast woodlands provided the charcoal necessary for smelting the ore. With a foothold, too, in the Cotswolds they were at the south-western end of the great Jurassic Way which led to the north-westwards, to Northamptonshire with its rich iron-stone, and to Lincolnshire and Yorkshire. We have already noticed an ironworking settlement at Hunsbury, Northamptonshire (map, p. 117), roughly half-way between the Iron Age 'B' settlers of the north-east and those of the south-west. And there was certainly some interchange of trade, and with it of ideas, along the Jurassic Way.

One of the most important discoveries of modern times has taken place in the Somerset Levels (marked 3 on the map on p. 86). To-day they are seldom more than a few feet above sea level and out of them rises the ridge of the Polden Hills and 'islands' such as Brent Knoll. In prehistoric times the Levels formed a large and shallow arm of the sea, so that Glastonbury Tor was at the head of a peninsula and the knoll was truly an island. Like that of the Fens of Norfolk and Lincolnshire the soil level has gradually been raised by slow accumulations of silt and peat, and later drainage has provided some of the richest grazing land in modern Britain.

But the peat did something more. It preserved the woodwork and basketry of Iron Age 'B' villagers who built their houses on islands that they had made for themselves in the shallow waters. Two of these villages are known, one just over a mile north-north-west of Glastonbury church, and the other less than a mile west-north-west of Meare church.

Once again let us call to our help the time machine and visit one of the villages in its heyday, in about the year A.D. one.

*

As we walk westward the Isle of Avalon is directly ahead and the line of the Mendip Hills rises to over 800 feet beyond shallow water on our right. To the left is the low ridge of the Polden Hills, also separated by water from the low and ever-narrowing neck of land along which our track passes. As we near the foot of Glastonbury Tor our way is barred by an earth wall, crowned by a wooden palisade that stretches to the water's edge on both sides of the track. The times are quiet and there is no guard to prevent our passing on through the narrow gateway with its empty guard-chambers. They are fast falling in, rotten to the heart-wood like the palisade itself. When next an enemy threatens all will have to be renewed in haste – perhaps too late to halt the enemy's rush.

We go on round the foot of the Tor and see before long,

amidst a watery wilderness, what looks like a floating African kraal of fifty or so round and domed thatched huts. Surrounding them is a stout palisade in good repair. To reach the village we go down to a causeway of quelchy timber and stone, greatly in need of repair, for the breakwater which shelters the causeway on the east has sunk so far that in rough weather angry wavelets break furiously against the path. On a spur of the causeway is a landing-stage of strong new logs beside which are moored several large dug-out canoes, some unloading merchandise which has come across the water from afar.

For this lake-village is a great trading centre and, so valuable is its merchandise, the founder-chieftains chose this spot to be safe from surprise attack by land or water. Lead from the Mendip mines is brought down on pack-animals by the track we have just trodden, and is shipped far and wide to customers. Tin comes in from Cornwall, worked shale from Dorset, glass beads from Gaul, amber by round-about routes from the west coast of Jutland, and iron from the Forest of Dean. The village stands near a meeting-place of routes by land and water.

The dense smoke rising from two of the outermost huts comes from furnaces which glow red when the clay-nosed bellows are brought to bear on the smouldering charcoal fire. Here, a smith is working in bronze, casting a scabbard which another craftsman will decorate with beautiful patterns. Another day he may cast tin or yet again lead, which he sometimes turns out as net-sinkers for the fishermen who contribute so much to the food of the place. Like the blacksmith nearby he is not allowed to set up shop in the

├─────── 29½" ───────┤

Early Iron Age 'B' currency bar of iron

middle of the village for fear he may set it all on fire. His own house has been burned down already several times.

The blacksmith, too, is busy. He is hammering out what seems to be a crude sword-blade. In fact it is a currency-bar, the money used by the merchants of the village. He is now making one of the largest size, though at other times he may be asked to produce any one of the six sizes in common demand by his customers. Seldom is he asked to make weapons, either spear or sword, for merchants avoid fighting whenever they can; it is bad for trade.

And it was this same smith who made the carpenter's tools (much like those in use in the twentieth century); and the carpenter, who is also the wheelwright and wainwright, built that heavy two-wheeled wagon that is now bumping along the causeway towards us, laden with broad baskets of threshed corn. So slow is the draught-ox that it has taken nearly the whole day to cart the load from the hill-side fields only five miles to the east. But the roughness of the unmade ways is largely to blame. It is well that the wright has used his best skill in making the wagon or it would have jolted to pieces long since.

The smell of sawdust and newly cut wood draws us to the carpenter, whose smaller wares, even, are so many that he has hardly room to work in his shop. Here is a nine-rung ladder of ash, a trough hollowed out of oak, and a barrel with staves so close-fitting that water cannot leak from it. The door of the shop itself is of solid wood well shaped, the upper and lower halves swinging separately each on its own hinges. At the moment the carpenter is finishing a wooden bowl at his pole-lathe in the corner. His son sits outside engraving on another bowl just such a pattern as we saw on the bronze scabbard. Even the potters love these compass-drawn designs and, though they do not know the use of the potter's wheel, they make most shapely vessels.

Further along, in an alley roughly cobbled with uneven stones, a hut is being rebuilt to replace one whose floor had sunk and become water-logged. The brushwood and timber foundations have already had to be renewed five times within living memory; that is the price the people pay for living safely in a marsh. The new clay floor and central hearth have already been laid down, and now walls of thick willow wands interwoven with wattle are being plaited like gigantic lobster pots. These will be daubed with clay to keep out wind and rain. Thatched on top with reeds, the house will be snug in winter when its heavy door is closed. But always the lapping of the water and the distant boom of the bittern will be heard through the long hours of the night.

Nearby is a cornstore on wooden stilts such as we saw at Little Woodbury, and, beyond it, blown hither and thither by the breeze, are the prettily-flecked feathers of a crane which a woman is plucking for the pot. Its grotesquely long legs jerk and flop back against the timbered floor as she turns it expertly to begin stripping the right wing. The feathers she stuffs deftly into a bag of woven grass; someone's bed will be the softer for them.

2¾"

Bone dice and box,
Glastonbury lake village

From the next hut comes the dull trundling sound of a small corn-mill worked by hand. The wheat flour, mixed with honey, the only sweetener, makes tasty cakes to carry on a day's fowling. Some of the men are just returning from the sport. Teal, widgeon, mallard, lordly heron, or humble moorhen – all make good eating to those who are hungry. Some are trapped in the decoy nets across the mere; others are brought down by clay bullets from a sling that is wielded with deadly accuracy.

Horses, sheep, pigs, cattle, and goats provide other meat that needs no catching, and the red and roe deer, especially in winter, provide yet different fare. The winter's feast is enlivened with stories of old battles and long voyages in search of new wares and new customers. When tongues and ears are tired, eyes are strained in the smoky gloom to see the fall of the dice; and stakes and tempers grow ever higher.

Things to be seen in the Open Air

The Danes' Graves (Marnian barrows) near Driffield, and mounds at Arras, Yorkshire; the cliff-castles, forts, villages, and fougous of Cornwall. Before excavation the lake villages appear merely as a group of hummocks.

In Museums

At Glastonbury and Taunton for objects from the lake villages. Harlyn Bay museum for burial groups. The British Museum, and The National Museum of Wales, Cardiff, for fine metal-work of the Iron Age 'B' people. Model of the lake village in Taunton Museum.

Warriors with Slings

As our story of prehistoric Britain proceeds we find the first clear light of history dawning. We begin to learn from accounts written at the time, or soon afterwards, the names of tribes and their customs and even, sometimes, the names of their chiefs. Already we have heard of the Parisii who settled in Yorkshire, and now we turn to another tribe against whom Julius Caesar made war and of whom he had many interesting things to say. In the last chapter we spoke of the cliff-castles of Cornwall, promontory forts in fact, bounded on all sides but one by the sea. Similar strongholds were known to Caesar on the southern coasts of Britanny, and he describes how difficult they were to storm. Their builders, the Veneti (who also gave their name to Venice, in Italy), were a great trading people, and they were probably involved in the Cornish tin trade long before Caesar knew them. They built massive oaken ships with leathern sails, which were seaworthy in the roughest weather. In his book, the *Commentaries*, Caesar describes a naval battle between his own war-galleys, low in the water, and the taller Venetic ships, which were too heavily built to be rammed in the usual Roman manner. In fact, it was a calm that defeated the Gauls. Having no oars, their ships were unable to escape the Roman galleys, which rowed to them in turn and fought a soldiers' battle across the decks. After the sea-fight Caesar punished the Veneti severely, and those that escaped from Roman slavery fled as refugees to the nearest coast of Britain (56 B.C.).

Besides their skill as sailors the Veneti had developed to a high degree the art of slinging stones. Their aim was effective at a hundred yards. And the refugees who came to southern Wessex and overcame the older Iron Age 'A' folk took over their hill-forts and greatly enlarged their defences. By far the most famous of these forts is Maiden Castle, near Dorchester, Dorset; and indeed, if I were asked for a list of the seven ancient wonders of Britain, Maiden Castle would be included with Stonehenge, Avebury, Silbury, Hadrian's Wall, Richborough Castle, and the Wansdyke.

At the time when the refugees arrived at Maiden Castle, the hill-top was already wrinkled with a long prehistory. Men of the New Stone Age had built a causewayed camp upon it, and along the crest of the hill they made a very long mound that may be a long barrow. But this was found only by excavation and cannot now be seen in the turf. Besides many small finds, including the crude figure of a goddess, a skeleton was discovered buried in disconnected fragments and with the skull broken open so that the brain could be eaten. This New Stone Age cannibal feast and subsequent burial was part of some religious ceremony that took place when the mound was made.

Apart from nearby round barrows, the men of the Bronze Age left no mark upon the great hill; but about three or four hundred years before Christ, Iron Age 'A' people built a fort with a single rampart and ditch on the eastern half of the hill. Part of this rampart can be seen on the aerial photographs which appear in most illustrated books of British prehistory. It runs across the middle of the far greater enclosure made by the later Iron Age people. After a time the whole of the hill-top was enclosed by a single ditch and rampart; and then, with the coming of the Veneti, the fort as we know it came into being (Pl. 9).

To-day we see it after two thousand years of slow wearing down by rain, frost and wind, and by the feet of men and animals. Yet words cannot convey its immensity; it must be seen and climbed over to be believed. Only the Wansdyke may be vaster; but the eye can take in only a little of that at a time, and three or four days are necessary to walk its whole length. Maiden Castle is fully five furlongs from east to west and more than two from north to south. If one stands at the bottom of one of the main ditches, the ramparts tower above to a height of sixty feet, and they stretch for two miles round the hill in three, four, and sometimes five great folds of earth. The ramparts alone cover some fifty acres of ground.

The fortress yielded many secrets during the wonderful excavations of the 1930s. One of them was the New Stone Age cannibalism mentioned earlier; another was the vast stores of carefully chosen sling bullets, 22,000 in one dump alone, that had been carted from the Chesil Beach, a place where pebbles are conveniently arranged by the waves in graded sizes. And it was the sling that made the multiple ramparts necessary, for in quantity the bullets must have been terrifying to an enemy whose effective range with the throwing spear was only thirty yards. Wooden platforms had existed near the guard-chambers at the gates, and from them the whole tortuous entry, twisting backwards and forwards through the outer horn works, could be covered with heavy and concentrated sling-fire. (In a simpler form is Almondbury, marked C in the diagram on p. 121.)

'The Belgae'

The last great prehistoric invasions were those of the Belgae, who began crossing from northern France and from Belgium about seventy-five years before Christ was born. Like the earlier Iron Age invaders of Britain and those of the Late Bronze Age, they were Celtic people; but the Belgae differed from earlier invaders in having intermarried with German tribes. Their language, however, remained a Celtic one (like those of Brittany, Wales, and Gaelic Scotland). Like earlier immigrants they moved westwards on the Continent because of the pressure of German tribes behind them; and the Germans would have begun to settle in Britain much earlier than they did if this island had not become a part of the Roman Empire. As it was, the German tribes, especially the Saxons, were carrying out piratical raids, often far inland, for at least two hundred years before they began settling down in eastern and southern Britain; and when they did come they ousted or enslaved those very people who had been a barrier to their south-westward advance and expansion on the Continent.

The Belgae were themselves the bravest fighters among the Gauls. One of their tribes, which had come from the Marne region and had seized much of south-eastern Britain by the time of Caesar's expedition of 55 B.C., was called the Catuvellauni (Mighty Warriors). Caesar found them true to their name when he fought against them.

As usually happened in prehistory (and in early history, too) the older inhabitants were not wiped out. The kinds of pottery they had used went on being made after the Belgic conquest. But the Belgae spread rapidly from Kent (map, overleaf), especially following the waterways through the forested areas, and, unlike earlier peoples, they sometimes settled in forest-clearings. Their methods of farming, particularly their use of a heavy plough, made it possible to work the heavier and richer soils of the forests which the older natives could not touch with their light ploughs.

Soon the Belgae set up a kingdom with its capital at Wheathampstead, four miles north of St Albans. There it is still possible to trace parts of the rampart which defended a town of a hundred acres; and there Cassivellaunus was king, 'the first man in England whose name we know'. From this town he led forth his army to fight against Julius Caesar's legions in 54 B.C. and back to it he returned pursued by the Romans. Caesar describes the stronghold as being protected by forest and marsh, and excellently fortified. Within it the Catuvellauni, tribesmen and cattle, had taken refuge in large numbers; but the place soon fell to the disciplined and fierce attack of the legions. Though many of the defenders escaped, many more were captured or killed, and many head of cattle were seized. Soon afterwards the Romans returned to Gaul, having gained little by their costly campaigns in Britain. It was not until a century later (A.D. 43) that the Roman conquest began in earnest.

Map showing the limits of Early Iron Age 'C' and the
territories of non-Belgic tribes

Later the Belgic capital was moved to Prae Wood, a mile
west of St Albans, just beyond the later Roman city, and
about this time Beech Bottom Dyke, a large earthwork just
north of the city, must have been dug, probably to mark a
boundary with another tribe. Finally, the Belgic capital was

138

established at Colchester in Essex, and remained so until the Roman conquest. Just outside Colchester in Lexden Park you may see a dyke like the one at Beech Bottom; and a whole system of them exists round the city of Chichester in Sussex.

Other states came into being, such as that of Commius, king of the Belgic Atrebates, who had been an ally of Caesar in Gaul and had then revolted against him. He fled to Britain in 51 B.C. and his sons set up their capital at Silchester among the heaths and woods of north Hampshire. Eventually, however, the Catuvellauni extended their sway until they controlled the whole of the south-east as far north as Cambridgeshire and Northamptonshire. The Atrebates eventually enlarged their territory until it took in Hampshire, Berkshire, and part of Wiltshire, and the tribe of the Regni in Sussex also came under their control.

Long before the Romans came to stay their influence was growing stronger in Britain. The Belgic kings struck coins inscribed sometimes with Roman lettering; Cunobelin, king of the Catuvellauni (the Cymbeline of Shakespeare's play) who died in A.D. 40, actually called himself *rex* (the Latin for 'king'); for the first time in Britain pottery began to be made on the wheel; and the main centres of population ceased to be on the hilltops as they had always been before. The Iron Age hill-fort and town at the Trundle (Goodwood) gave place to the first city of Chichester on the plain; Winchester began at

(A) Belgic gold coin; (B) Iron Age 'C' (Belgic) pedestal urn

a time soon after the desertion of the fortress on St Catherine's Hill, just south of the mediaeval city; and there are other probable instances of a change of settlement sites from higher to lower ground.

The real reason for this is bound up with the change in farming methods mentioned earlier. The Belgae had the implements suitable for cultivating the richer lowland soils, and they built their dwellings close to their fields. As these were situated in areas that have been farmed almost ever since their days, traces of their field boundaries have not been identified, mainly because they have been destroyed by later ploughing. It is very likely, however, that they ploughed long strips as the Saxons were to do five hundred years later; and it may be that some of the strip lynchets now called Saxon have in fact a longer history. Certainly air-photographs of the Fens in Cambridgeshire and Lincolnshire show strip fields; and in one place eleven miles north-east of Peterborough, there is a settlement with a Roman road making a marked detour in its straight course in order to avoid the houses and fields. These must therefore have existed before the road was built. Romano-British sherds are to be found on the surface, and the fields stretch for some distance to the north-east of the settlement.

Caesar's conquest of Gaul, complete by about 51 B.C., made possible new trade routes from the Mediterranean countries to Britain. The wealth of the Belgic lords, which came from their improved agriculture, enabled them to buy quantities of goods, especially food-oils and wines, which were brought in big jars called *amphorae* (see p. 155, C). These jars have been found in the tombs of several Belgic chiefs of eastern England. With them have been found costly pots from Italy and silver goblets from Gaul. These luxuries were paid for in gold coins, and partly through the export of metals and of agricultural products. A lively export trade in slaves is indicated by many finds of the chains in which they were sent to market.

Certainly south-eastern Britain began to take on a new importance at this time. It offered the rich soils upon which

Belgic wealth was founded, and was closest to the Roman provinces on the Continent with which so much trade was carried on. With the foundation of London in early Roman times the importance of south-eastern Britain was confirmed, and except for a time at the end of the Roman period and in early Saxon times, the south-east continued to grow in importance and strength until it finally dominated the whole of the British Isles.

Salisbury Plain, the capital region of prehistoric Britain, steadily lost its old importance. It is true that until late in the Roman period the chalk uplands of Wessex continued to be cultivated by a large population of peasants living in hamlets and solitary farmsteads. Their field-boundaries can still be traced over large areas on the chalk even to-day (see p. 98) because the Saxons preferred to plough the valley soils and merely pastured their cattle on the downlands. But from the first century B.C. the Plain began to lose its old importance. The wealthy Britons of the Belgic and Roman periods set up their farms (called 'villas') round the fringes of Salisbury Plain on the richer soils. Towards the end of the Roman period there are indications that parts of the Plain and of Cranborne Chase went out of cultivation and became a vast sheep pasture. Here and there villas have been found which had largely ceased to be farmhouses and had become factories for the cleaning of woollen cloth, but the main centre of this industrial process was at Winchester where a government factory was set up.

When the Romans began their conquest of Britain they found the south-east heavily populated by a highly civilized people much like the Gauls across the Channel. As the legions fought their way farther north and west they met tribes less and less civilized, living a kind of life that had been usual in the south-east many centuries before. Had the Romans not arrived on the scene there is little doubt that the

Belgae would have conquered all the tribes right up to the limits of the highland zone. (See the map on p. 86.)

Much has been learned of the Belgae from their burials. The corpse was always cremated, and for the poorer people a simple hole up to a yard across was dug and the ashes put in it. Sometimes a number of these burials are found arranged in a rough circle. Usually each of the pits contains only one or two of the typical pedestal urns, one of them containing the burnt bones (see p. 139). Chiefs, however, were accompanied by much finer grave-goods, and sometimes the burial was made in a large vault with elaborate cooking equipment and implements for the ceremonial sacrifice of animals. In a burial at Lexden Park near Colchester the remains of a chariot and chain-armour, studded with silver, were found.

This last, and several other burials of Belgic princes, were made under tall conical barrows. These continued to be constructed during the Roman period (see diagram below) by the native chiefs, and are usually to be seen near or close

Roman barrow

alongside Roman roads. They are called 'Roman' barrows, but they are Roman only in the sense that they were made during the Roman period. (Pl. 12b.)

Things to be seen in the Open Air

Belgic or Roman barrows such as those beside the Roman road at Badbury Rings, Dorset; the Six Hills at Stevenage, Hertfordshire, and the Bartlow Hills, Cambridgeshire. Belgic earthworks near St Albans, Colchester, Silchester, and Chichester. The

Wheathampstead defences. The Belgic settlement in Prae Wood, near St Albans. Belgic strip fields on Twyford Down, just south of Winchester.

In Museums

Especially those of south-east England; in the British Museum, the Verulamium, Maidstone, and Colchester Museums in particular, are to be seen many kinds of objects from Belgic sites.

6: The Roman Occupation of Britain

IT would be altogether impossible to give an account of the Roman conquest and occupation of Britain in a single chapter or even in several chapters. The facts may be gained from a number of books, few of them easy reading, that may be borrowed from a public library. But a few matters of general importance will be mentioned here to explain some of the more interesting things that you may come across in the field.

The first important thing to understand is that the Roman conquest was not followed by the arrival of large numbers of Romans who settled down in Britain. In fact, apart from soldiers and officials, there were very few Romans in this country. Even the army in later times was mainly recruited from Gaul and Germany, and in the later days of the Empire even the highest commander might be a barbarian (that is, one who was not a Roman).

The first thing the Romans did after landing in new territory was to construct a safe base to which fresh supplies of men and materials could be brought and landed, and to which the army might retreat when in difficulties. Caesar made a camp which enclosed all the several hundreds of ships which had transported his second expedition to Britain in 54 B.C., and the work occupied his soldiers for ten days and nights.

When the Romans came to conquer in A.D. 43 they landed to the north of the earlier camp, near the present Richborough, and fortified a headland by cutting a double ditch across its base. The part of this work that lies within the later Roman fort can be seen by visitors to the place, together with the camp with three lines of ditches built about A.D. 250. The stone ramparts and bastions, which are so wonderfully preserved, were put up some twenty-five years later still (A.D. 275). There is much else to see at Richborough surviving from the Roman period, and anyone spending a holiday at a resort in east Kent will find plenty of interest in the fort and in the objects from it now shown in the museum there. Very early remains similar to those at Richborough have been excavated near Colchester, and this city, too, has a fine museum of Belgic as well as Roman goods.

The main opposition to the legions came from the Belgic tribes of the south-east. Others, like the Iceni of Norfolk and the Regni of Sussex, gave what help they could to the Romans against the hated Belgae. As the invading armies moved north and west they built marching camps wherever they halted for the night. Many of these have survived from the later campaigns in northern England and Scotland, and many fine air photographs can be seen of them in many recent books on archaeology. A few camps have recently been found in southern England and the Cotswolds, and air survey may be expected to increase the known number of them. A fine one, which about A.D. 45 became a garrison

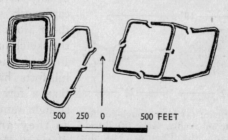

500   250   0   500 FEET

Roman Britain. Plans of Roman camps,
Cawthorn, Yorks, N. Riding

camp, may be seen in one corner of the great Iron Age fort of Hod Hill north of Blandford, Dorset. Others are known at Ashley, near King's Somborne, Hants, at Easton Grey near Malmesbury, Wilts, and at Greensforge, twelve miles west of Birmingham. One or two others are known in Kent and other counties (map, p. 162). If you look at the Ordnance Survey map of Roman Britain you can locate the sites of many more in northern Britain and

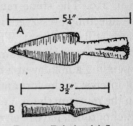

Roman Britain: (A) Iron spearhead, Hod Hill, Dorset; (B) Iron catapult dart

two together south-east of Llandovery in Wales. Do not be misled by names like 'Caesar's Camp' on modern maps, or by 'Roman Camp' on older maps; these are usually forts of the Early Iron Age. A Roman camp almost always has straight sides and rounded corners, with one or more ditches round the rampart. The entrances in the middle of the sides usually have a small earthwork defending them (look back at the sketch on p. 145). Few of the earlier hill-forts have more than a few yards of straight rampart, and so they are easily distinguished from Roman camps.

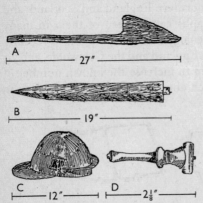

Roman Britain: (A) Iron plough-coulter, Great Witcombe villa, Glos; (B) Broadsword blade, the Thames, Fulham; (C) Helmet of legionary soldier, London; (D) First-century brooch, London

By the year A.D. 47 the Romans reached a line which stretches from Seaton in Devon via Bath, Cirencester, and Leicester to Lincoln (map, p. 162), and they established it as a temporary frontier. They built a road along it, chiefly for patrol purposes, and most of it is still in use. Where it remains as a mere footpath or cart-track its original form is easy to understand; for long stretches, however, it has been re-made as a broad trunk road with all its original characteristics blotted out. Even so, where the modern road wanders from the straight line, and no natural obstacle such as a steep-sided valley is the cause of the deviation, the original bank of the Roman road may sometimes be found following the straight line that the modern road has left.

Throughout England, but especially in the South and East, many stretches of Roman road still remain to be found and added to the map. In order to find out what they look like it is necessary to follow a good known stretch across open country. Many of the One-Inch Ordnance Survey sheets show disused sections, but probably the best is the Ackling Dyke, from a point one and a half miles south of Bishopstone in south Wiltshire, to Badbury Rings four miles north-west of Wimborne Minster, Dorset. This is to be found on sheets 167 and 179 of the New Popular Edition of the maps, and along its route, and within easy reach of the road on both sides, are many fine examples of prehistoric earthworks (map, p. 56). It is fine country for walking or cycling.

The present appearance of a Roman road is not very exciting, yet the work of tracing one, in spite of many disappointments and even total failure, grows in interest with the growth of knowledge and experience of field work. A long, generally straight, low green bank (*agger*) rising in a gentle curve to the middle, is what you will first notice. Then you may see hollows on each side of it for drainage or from which the material of the *agger* was taken. Often the road has been robbed in recent centuries to make another nearby, and the old road then presents a very bumpy appearance. Where a cart-track cuts through it you may sometimes find a good section whose make-up can be studied.

In the highland zone, where gravel was often hard to come by, the road was sometimes paved with slabs of stone. A fine example of this type of construction is to be seen on Blackstone Edge about fifteen miles north-east of Manchester and from two to four miles east of Littleborough, south of the modern road. This stretch survives as a paved way about fifteen feet wide hemmed in between kerbstones sunk well into the ground. Down the centre of the road is a hollow which may have been worn by the skid-pans of wagons on their way down. The hooves of draught animals produce the same effect to-day on gravelly or chalky cart-tracks. Another fine stretch of paved road is to be seen at Goathland on Wheeldale Moor, nine miles south-east of Whitby, Yorkshire. This road leads to the well-preserved temporary Roman marching camps at Cawthorn (see diagram on p. 145).

A little to the west and north of the Fosse Way, and at varying distances from it, is the boundary-line between the highland and lowland zones (map, p. 86), and in Roman times these two regions continued to be as different as they had always been during prehistory.

In the highland zone, that is in Devon and Cornwall, in Wales, the Pennines, and the North, Roman ideas and habits made little impression. In some parts of the highland zone life changed hardly at all between 1000 B.C. and A.D. 1000. Even in some parts of the lowland zone the natives continued to live as they had before the coming of the Romans; the only important change was that the tribes were prevented from warring with each other.

But whereas in the highland zone almost all Roman remains are military – camps, forts, walls, signal stations, and strategic roads – in the lowlands of the South and East the remains consist of towns (chiefly their walls) and of large farms (the villas). In both zones relics of the mass production of pottery are found, though it is in the lowlands that most of these industrial centres were situated. In the Weald of Sussex and in the Forest of Dean iron was mined and smelted; in Cornwall tin continued to be produced. Only in the later Roman period, when Britain was being attacked by barbarians from all sides, were military forces normally garrisoned in the lowlands, and coastal forts and town walls were built to guard against these savage raiders (map, p. 162).

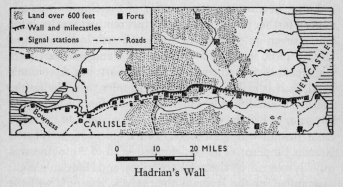

Hadrian's Wall

The history and design of Hadrian's Wall, the northern frontier of the Roman Empire, is far too complicated to describe in one or two paragraphs, and those who want a fuller but simple account of it should obtain *Ancient Monuments: Northern England* (1951: Her Majesty's Stationery Office, 3s. 6d.). Like all the other volumes in this series this is wonderful value for the money, and describes and illustrates monuments of all ages down to modern times.

The Wall runs for seventy-three and a half miles from Wallsend (Newcastle-on-Tyne) on the North Sea to Bowness-on-Solway on the Irish Sea. It was built from A.D. 122–6 or a little later, but during construction the plan was altered, and it is not the same throughout. At every Roman mile (equal to one thousand paces) a small mile-castle was built, and between the mile-castles two turrets were placed as look-out posts. To the south of the Wall was a military road, and still farther south the *Vallum* was made: a broad ditch with the earth cast up on both sides of it. At irregular intervals along the Wall were a number of larger forts in which legionaries were garrisoned, and from which they could be rushed along the military road to those parts of the Wall nearest to their fort when danger threatened.

Later, in A.D. 142, the frontier of the Empire was advanced farther to the north, and a turf rampart was built for thirty-seven miles from the Firth of Forth to the Firth of Clyde. This, too, had a ditch in front and nineteen forts connected by a road south of the rampart; but Antonine's Wall, as it is called, is altogether simpler than Hadrian's. It had a useful life of less than fifty years, for in A.D. 197 the governor of Britain, Clodius Albinus, took most of the army from Britain with him to Gaul in a bid to make himself Roman Emperor. The undefended Wall of Antonine was quickly overrun by the northern tribes, and Hadrian's Wall, dismantled by the Romans themselves, was now without its garrison. Able to work at their leisure, the northern barbarians wrecked it in about A.D. 198 as thoroughly as they could, and went as far south as York and Chester, destroying and pillaging as they went. Hadrian's Wall was soon restored, but the Picts from the North swept across it again and again in the later days of the Roman occupation whenever its garrison was drawn away to fight elsewhere.

The three great fortresses of York, Chester, and Caerleon

(see map on p. 162) were carefully placed for military reasons. Each was planned as the permanent base for a legion (5,000 to 6,000 troops), York for the North, Chester for the North-west and to guard the coastal route into North Wales, and Caerleon ('Camp of the Legion' is its meaning) to cover the southern coastal route into Wales. The Devon-Cornwall peninsula was too thinly populated to need a permanent military centre; its tribes could offer no serious threat to Roman rule. Within the walls of these fortresses were barracks, officers' quarters, food-stores, workshops, and a hospital. York can still show fragments of the curtain wall and also the 'Multangular Tower' which formed the western bastion of the legionary fortress. Close to the Tower is the Yorkshire Museum, with many Roman exhibits. The Tower, in fact, represents a vast rebuilding that took place throughout the North, on Hadrian's Wall and in the many forts, after their destruction by the Picts in about the year 296. These marauders were once again able to cross the frontier in force because the Roman garrisons had been withdrawn to the south by the general Allectus who, like Clodius before him, was seeking to become Emperor. He too was killed, defeated in the attempt.

At Chester, as at York, Lincoln, and Caerleon, the first legionary fortress was of earth and timber, and excavations suggest that it was built between A.D. 60 and 80. Thirty or so years later building in stone began and, as at York, there was much work of reconstruction in the early part of the third century. The walls of the mediaeval city of Chester remain almost complete, and in the north-west angle near the Cathedral they are built on a Roman base. Near the East Gate is the amphitheatre, where soldiers and civilians of the fortress found their entertainment. This, and the Grosvenor Museum, which has much material on show from the Roman city of Chester, should certainly not be missed.

The third great fortress, Caerleon, is situated by the river Usk three miles north-east of Newport, Monmouthshire. Not much of the site has been covered by later building so that, besides the remains of an amphitheatre, the foundations of a bath-house outside the ramparts and of important buildings towards the centre of the fort help one to picture its original appearance. The ramparts themselves stand to a height of twelve feet in places.

Of the more purely civilian towns of Roman Britain several have not been built upon since they were deserted in the fourth or fifth century, and consequently excavation has made it possible to learn much more about them than about those now covered with mediaeval and modern buildings. But ever since they were deserted the ramparts and buildings have been steadily robbed of stone and brick, so that often only foundations survive to-day; and these remain only because they were buried out of reach of the robbers.

Nine miles east of Caerleon lie the remains of the civilian town of Caerwent. It was the capital of the tribe called the Silures, who had been removed from the near-by hill-fort of Llanmelin to the new Roman town in about A.D. 75. This at first was protected by a clay bank and double ditches, but later, in about A.D. 200, the raids of Irish pirate-bands made it necessary to construct a stone rampart. Even this proved insufficient, and in the fourth century bastion-towers were added on which catapults could be mounted as artillery. Perhaps at the same time the broad southern gate was blocked with stone-work to make defence easier. This blocking can still be seen. Within the walls was a chess-board pattern of streets and blocks of buildings; and in the middle of the town were situated the Senate House of the Silures, public baths, a temple, and a colonnaded market place. In the surrounding blocks were private houses, shops, and inns. Towards the end of its life *Venta Silurum* (its ancient name) was provided with an amphitheatre, though it is a poor thing compared with the one at Caerleon. Many of the objects found are in the Newport Museum, and some others can be seen in the church at Caerwent. The museum at Caerleon is also worth a visit. The regional guide, *Ancient Monuments: South Wales and Monmouthshire* (1950: Her Majesty's Stationery Office, 3s. 6d.) contains much interesting information about Caerleon and Caerwent, as well as about other Roman and earlier and later sites in the region.

Of the other cities of Roman Britain, whether they are open sites like Wroxeter (five miles south-east of Shrewsbury), Caistor-by-Norwich, Silchester (six miles north of Basingstoke, Hampshire), or have modern cities built over them like London, Canterbury, Cirencester, Chichester, Gloucester, Exeter, Dorchester, Leicester, or Lincoln, all have some relic or other in the open or accessible beneath modern buildings, and all preserve many articles of Roman everyday use in the local museums. To understand what these places looked like and how their inhabitants lived you must go to a museum; the best of them, like the one at Verulamium, give vivid impressions of these things.

London has fragments of the Roman wall and of the bastions, and especially fine is the section to be seen near St Giles, Cripplegate. As in many other places, the Roman work provided a good foundation for the fortifications of the Middle Ages. Bath can show one of the buildings that gave the city its English name. Lincoln, besides fragments of its walls and part of the defending ditch, has the Newport Gate through which traffic still passes. Much of the same kind survives at Colchester and, in addition, beneath the Norman castle (now a museum), are the remains of a vast early temple. Perhaps Verulamium is the most rewarding of Roman cities, and in its visible remains links the distant past with the present in the most fascinating way.

The Roman city lies between the Belgic settlement in Prae Wood and the mediaeval city with its enormously long cathedral, built largely from bricks prised from the structures of the Roman town. So complete was this robbing that little remains above ground; but excavations in the 1930s and more recently have provided a great wealth of information about it, and some of the buildings have been left uncovered for inspection. There is a good section of the rampart (Pl. 11a), the foundations of a main city gate, tessellated pavements, *hypocausts* (heating systems of houses), and a very fine theatre (Pl. 11b).

Vast areas of forest remained throughout Britain during this period, but the Belgae and their Romanized descendants were beginning to nibble at its fringes. The iron industry of the Weald, which had come into being not long before the Roman conquest, required constant and heavy fellings to provide the charcoal fuel for smelting. At a number of places in central and eastern Sussex heaps of slag, with stray Roman potsherds and coins, remained until modern times as evidence of the industry. Beauport Park (Westfield), Chitcombe (Broad Oak), and Footlands (near Mountfield) are among the sites of Roman iron-smelting works. There are, no doubt, others still to be found in the Weald and in the Forest of Dean; but most of the slag-heaps that survive are the result of the smelting of mediaeval and early modern times. The many hammer-ponds of Sussex and Surrey are also relics of the later industry.

The slag was not altogether waste. It was used in the making of Roman roads, at least three of which crossed the Weald from north to south, and which were made to transport the products of the furnaces. Mr I. D. Margary has written a splendid book about these and other roads in the South-east called *Roman Ways in the Weald*. From it you may learn a great deal about the work of the archaeological

detective and about field work generally. At Holtye, near
East Grinstead, you can see a hundred yards' length of one
of these 'iron' roads, uncovered by Mr Margary and main-
tained by the Sussex Archaeological Trust; and in the
Forest of Dean, two miles north-west of Blakeney, at Black-
pool Bridge, there is a paved road with kerbs along which
the iron from the Dean mines was transported. Even more
remarkable is the Roman iron mine in Lydney Park, a place
which has several other antiquities to show. I shall speak of
them later.

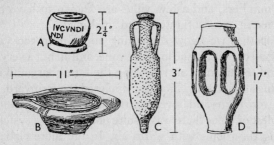

Roman Britain: (A) Ink-pot, London; (B) Food mortar,
London; (C) Amphora (wine jar), Welwyn, Herts;
(D) Roman beaker pot, Colchester

Another flourishing industry was pot-making. This, too,
needed abundant wood fuel, and suitable clay; the forested
regions usually afforded both. Many pottery kilns have been
found in the New Forest and near Upchurch on the south
side of the Medway estuary. Another important centre of
manufacture was Castor, Northamptonshire, which sold
its wares over a wide area. Pottery sites are usually detected
by the finding of many 'wasters': pieces of pots that have
sagged, cracked, or broken when being fired in the kiln, or
when cooling afterwards. If a kiln was in use for a long time
vast quantities of wasters accumulated in dumps. Under
the fallen leaves in Alice Holt Forest near Farnham,

Hampshire, large areas of soil are littered with these rejects from Roman kilns.

A few of the Roman villas became factories, at any rate towards the end of their period of use. Excavated examples which can be seen at Chedworth (Gloucestershire), Titsey (Surrey), and Darenth (Kent) were employed in the fulling (cleansing and thickening) of cloth. Natural fuller's earth, necessary in the process, is found near the Chedworth Villa and within ten miles of the one at Titsey. At Ashtead in Surrey tiles bearing the maker's trademark were made in large numbers, and a few villas are known to have been occupied in iron-working or lead smelting.

Altogether we know something about over 500 villas, almost all of them in the lowland zone, and all but a very few devoted to farming. Surrounding the farmhouse and outbuildings was a wall which also enclosed the farmyard, and there were barns and hovels for the labourers. In all but the humblest of villas there was a suite of baths and a system of heating the rooms with warm air. In the more elaborate villas as many as twenty rooms may be found, some of which may be floored with patterns of tiny coloured stones known as tessellated pavements. Some windows were filled with

Reconstruction of the late second-century villa at Park Street, near St Albans, Herts

glass, and the walls of the rooms were often covered with plaster with patterns painted on it. The standard of comfort enjoyed by their inhabitants was probably higher than was known in this country until quite recent times; indeed, many people to-day live in much greater discomfort in winter than these native country gentlemen of Roman times.

Most of the villa rooms were grouped round a courtyard reached directly from the farmyard, and the courtyard was surrounded by a veranda from which the rooms could be entered. Many of the villas underwent one or more rebuildings, but few of them survived the terrible barbarian raids of the year 367. Not many of them were actually destroyed at this time, but the owner probably fled to the safety of the nearest town and left his slaves to produce as much as they would. Even the slaves may have revolted, and made life in the countryside very dangerous. At any rate, a few villas seem to have been burned down at about this time, and many more began to fall into ruin. In only a few do the finds of coins and pottery indicate that normal life went on in the villas after 367.

There were other, less destructive attacks by Picts, Saxons, or Franks both before and after the year 367, and a few villas are known to have been fortified with an earthen bank and ditch as a protection against small bodies of these raiders. North-west of Woodstock, Oxfordshire, an area of twenty-two square miles is enclosed by a protective bank called the Grim's Ditch, and within it the sites of at least six villas are known. This Grim's Ditch was dug by the Belgae, but the villas enjoyed its protection, and other earthwork fortifications were built round some of the villas and are still plain to see. At Ely, near Cardiff, a villa was surrounded by a bank and ditch in about the year 300, but it was attacked and destroyed only twenty-five years later. Only a few miles to the north-west the Llantwit Major villa, which had no protection, was sacked and the inhabitants butchered in about 305 by Irish pirates. Similar instances of burning and massacre are known from the lowland zone.

The villas are seldom discovered on the uplands; there, instead, the farming hamlets (Pl. 16b) of the Early Iron Age continued their cultivation of the small, squarish 'Celtic' fields that were described in Chapter 4 (see p. 98). The influence of Roman life was scarcely felt in these peasant homes. A few of the more prosperous farmers could afford to have the walls of their houses covered with painted plaster, and coins, good pottery, and some metal goods could be obtained by the richer peasants, especially in southern England. The kilns for drying corn found in the farmsteads of Cranborne Chase are not usually found elsewhere.

From this same region comes most of the evidence for a change from corn-growing to sheep-farming in the later Roman period. Attached to some of the farmsteads are straight-sided enclosures which would have served well for sheep-folds. A very good example can be seen on Knighton Hill, Broad Chalke; and a kite-shaped enclosure on Rockbourne Down, three miles to the south-east, is certainly of the late Roman period. Rather farther to the south is the so-called Soldiers' Ring, near South Damerham, whose banks run across 'Celtic' fields which must obviously have gone out of cultivation before the enclosure was made. These three sites are to be found on the map on p. 56, the first near the top in the middle, the second half-way down the right-hand edge of the map, and the third just above the key to the map.

In the lowland zone stone could not easily be obtained for building at this time, but in the highland regions it was commonly used, and earthworks are therefore uncommon.

In Cornwall the stone-built villages at Chysauster and elsewhere continued to be occupied during the Roman period, and in Wales there is no very remarkable change in village life between the Early Iron Age and later times. A native settlement at Din Lligwy in the Isle of Anglesey has an enclosing stone wall with five straight sides in the Roman manner, and it has oblong as well as round buildings inside. And the hill-fort of Tre'r Ceiri in Caernarvonshire is defended by a rampart with a wall-walk on top of it which is Roman in appearance. But the outline of the fort is very irregular and hardly one of the dwellings inside it has a straight wall.

When raiding became common a number of the older hill-top forts, like Dinorben near Abergele, were brought back into use and became bases for the local soldiers. But Roman power in Wales came to an end in 383, when the governor of Britain, Magnus Maximus, withdrew the legions to fight for him in Gaul. Hadrian's Wall was abandoned at the same time for the same reason.

Among the most remarkable monuments to Roman engineering skill are the canals for drainage and transport still traceable in East Anglia and Lincolnshire. The Car Dyke can be traced for most of its five-mile length from the river Cam at Waterbeach, Cambridgeshire, to a junction with the Old West River near Haddenham. Just north of Cottenham it skirts the remains of a Romano-British village, and it is in this neighbourhood that the canal survives at its best. A similar canal, bearing the same name, runs from the river Nen at Peterborough for sixty miles with little deviation to the river Witham below Lincoln. To the west of that city is another stretch, called the Foss Dyke, linking the Witham with the river Trent at Torksey, a distance of nine miles.

A very different kind of site to be found here and there is the shrine or temple of a native or Roman god. Several small native temples have been found, including one that had to be destroyed at Heathrow when London Airport was being constructed. At Farley Heath in Surrey and at Maiden Castle in Dorset, however, the foundations of shrines have been left open for all to see. In the larger cities quite imposing buildings were erected: at Bath to the goddess Sul Minerva, in London to Isis, and in Colchester to the Emperor Claudius deified. Of these nothing remains above ground, but at Colchester the vaults of the temple can still be entered beneath the Norman castle. Yet the most remarkable Roman temple-site in Britain is that at Lydney, Gloucestershire. It stands within an Iron Age fort and near to the Roman iron mine. It was dedicated to the Celtic god Nodens, and near it was a large inn for pilgrims to the shrine, as well as a bathhouse and what seems to have been a row of shops. The foundations of these buildings are on view, and so are many objects found during the excavations on the site.

Of a very different kind is the sacred site at Cerne Abbas in Dorset. Cut in outline in the chalk is a giant figure, perhaps a representation of Hercules, and above his head, on the top of the hill, is a small square embanked enclosure where, no doubt, ceremonies in his honour were held. The Long Man of Wilmington in Sussex has certainly suffered much alteration and his origin is consequently unknown. Recently it has been suggested that he was graven in Saxon times, for he is similar to a figure embossed on one of the plates attached to the helmet from the famous ship-burial of Sutton Hoo, Suffolk. And, while speaking of hill-figures, the White Horse at Uffington, Berkshire, must be mentioned. It is situated very near to the Iron Age fort of Uffington Castle, and the White Horse is very like the disjointed horses stamped on Iron Age coins (see p. 139), so it may be that the Uffington figure belongs to that period too. The many other figures cut into the chalk turf of the downlands

The Uffington White Horse

are all modern, though one or two may overlie ancient work which is now lost for ever.

As the Roman grip on Britain grew weaker, enemies from north, east, and west became bolder and raided farther inland. The military leaders did all that was possible to hold the barbarian raiders in check. As we saw, Hadrian's Wall was rebuilt in about A.D. 300, after its destruction by the Picts. Later in the same century bastions were added to the walls of London and Caerwent. But it was of little use to check the raiders when they had already penetrated far inland. The most effective defence was to attack them at sea as they approached the coast. And so heavily fortified coastal bases were established from which naval squadrons could operate against the German pirates who so often swept across the North Sea in search of plunder.

From the Wash to the Isle of Wight, round half our east and south coasts, may still be seen the vast ruins of the forts of the Saxon Shore; and at Cardiff Castle, at Caernarvon, and at Holyhead in Anglesey are fragments of forts defending the West in a similar manner against Irish pirates. In England, those at Burgh (Suffolk, Pl. 14), Reculver and Richborough (Kent), Pevensey (Sussex), and Portchester (Hampshire) (map, p. 162) are especially worth a visit, and as all of them are within easy reach of popular holiday resorts, the opportunity to visit one or other of them comes to most people at some time. The descriptive pamphlets

Map of the visible remains of the Roman period

published by the Ministry of Works and costing only a penny or two, should be bought for the better understanding of the places. In fact the short guides to all the ancient monuments in the care of the Ministry are excellent value for the money and should never be missed.

Things to be seen in the Open Air

A representative selection of the many hundreds of Roman sites has been given already in this chapter; a few Roman villas that have not been covered again after excavation may, however, be found useful: Lockleys, near Welwyn, Hertfordshire; Bignor, Angmering, and Southwick (all Sussex); Titsey (Surrey); Brading (Isle of Wight); King's Weston, Spoonley, and Wadfield (nr. Winchcomb); Chedworth (Gloucestershire); Wraxall and Keynsham (Somerset); North Leigh (Oxfordshire); Grimston (Norfolk).

In Museums

Almost every local museum has some interesting material on show. The following show models that are valuable in giving a clear idea of the original appearance of certain buildings: Verulamium Museum: the 'London' gate of the city; a potter's kiln; and later there will be a model of the whole Roman city. Salisbury Museum: potter's kiln in New Forest. Pitt-Rivers Museum (Farnham, Dorset): a 'villa' at Iwerne; native villages and burials. These models show the methods of excavation. The Science Museum, London (Children's Gallery): models of a villa with its heating system, and of a potter's kiln. National Museum of Wales, Cardiff: model of Caerleon fort. Grosvenor Museum, Chester: model of the city and surroundings; fully-armed figure of a Roman soldier.

7: After the Romans

By the time the Romans left Britain in A.D. 410 the towns were already in ruins and very few of the villas can have been carrying on as they were intended. Even the roads gradually became less and less usable, for there was no one who troubled to repair them. For long into the Dark Ages they continued to be used by men and beasts of burden, but there were probably no wheeled vehicles to be jolted to pieces on their bumpy surfaces. Some of them never went out of use, because they linked places that continued to be important. The Watling Street from Canterbury to London is certainly one of them, and there are sections of others that never lost their usefulness however uneven their surfaces became.

It is likely that a small Roman army returned to Britain for a few years in the early fifth century, but the evidence is not very clear, and in any case is found only in the South-east. Between 400 and 450 there is an almost complete blank in archaeology. Some very tiny coins (fifty of them can be placed without overlapping on a halfpenny) were found at Lydney and Verulamium to show that a spark of life remained in those places. At Lydney, and at Yarnbury camp in Wiltshire, and Cissbury in Sussex, the defensive ramparts were strengthened at some time in this period. It is likely, too, that some of the earthworks near Silchester in Hampshire were constructed at this time. The Grim's Dyke at Pinner in Middlesex, and the *Faestendic* (fortress ditch) near Bexley, Kent, may also have been made to mark the outer limits of the territory that a shrunken London regarded as its own.

But we cannot expect much to remain from this twilit time between the Roman and Saxon Periods. Almost everywhere the soil which may have contained evidence of it has been so disturbed by ploughing that scarcely anything survives to be discovered. And, in any case, it seems that ordinary metalcraft was nearly extinct and that the making of pottery was generally so crude that sherds cease to be recognizable owing to their disintegration in moist soil. Life was on the whole more primitive than it had been before the Romans came.

The first English bands are said to have come soon after A.D. 450 as allies of the Britons to protect them against the Picts and Scots. But soon they rebelled against their allies, and scattered bands of Angles, Saxons, and Jutes began settling in all those regions where the soil is good and that could be reached easily from the North Sea and the eastern part of the English Channel. We know of the places chosen for their villages only from the many discoveries of their burial-places. The earliest of these have been found in East Yorkshire, Lincolnshire, East Anglia, Kent, Sussex, and on the south bank of the Thames in Berkshire.

Before the English crossed the seas to Britain they had been accustomed to burn their dead and to bury the ashes in an urn. After their settlement in England they slowly changed over to the custom of burying the body unburned. With it they put those possessions that had been most treasured during life – a man's weapons and accoutrements or a woman's jewels. It is from these objects that we have learned much of what we now know about our early ancestors. Sometimes, when a person was cremated, his or her possessions were not burned with the body but were later put with the ashes in the cremation urn. Usually, however, the objects found in urns are so bent and twisted that they are scarcely recognizable. This shows that they were put on the funeral pyre with the corpse.

Fashions in pottery, jewellery, and weapons were constantly changing, though certainly not as rapidly as fashions change to-day. These changes in grave-goods make it possible to distinguish between earlier and later burials, and sometimes between cremations of different centuries. Some of the objects found in cremation pots or with skeletons are so like others found in north Germany, Holland, or Denmark, where the English tribes formerly lived, that it is possible to say that they were buried with some of the earliest English invaders of this island. And those same objects, when found in several places in England and on the Continent, may indicate the route taken by some of the first invaders, and the region from which they started out. For example, the equal-armed brooch (see figure c opposite) has been found in cremation urns in north Germany, and with skeletons or cremations in Cambridgeshire, Bedfordshire, and Berkshire. It suggests that invaders from Old Saxony (in north Germany) crossed the North Sea to the Wash, and first by the rivers, and then along the Icknield Way, they spread south-westwards across central England. So you see, these brooches not only suggest the route taken, but also the tribe to which these settlers belonged.

The goods buried with the dead can be seen in museums (and see drawing opposite); in the open air there are very few remains surviving from the time before the English became Christians and began burying their dead in a graveyard without their worldly possessions. From 450, when they first began settling here, until the seventh century, when they accepted Christianity, the great majority of Anglo-Saxons were buried in flat graves with only a low mound of earth displaced by the body to indicate its position. This is just what you see in a churchyard still, but the earliest of

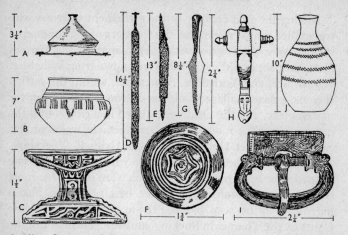

Anglian, Saxon, and Jutish objects: (A) Iron shield-boss, the Thames, Brentford; (B) Anglo-Frisian pot, fifth century, Caythorpe, Lincs; (C) Saxon bronze equal-armed brooch of about A.D. 450, Kempston, Beds; (D) Iron sword, Mitcham, Surrey; (E) Typical Saxon knife (scramasax); (F) Saxon gilt-bronze saucer brooch, about A.D. 500, Mitcham, Surrey; (G) Iron spearhead, Ewell, Surrey; (H) Anglian bronze cruciform brooch of about A.D. 500, West Stow Heath, Suffolk; (I) Bronze buckle, about A.D. 500, Long Wittenham, Berks; (J) Jutish or Frankish bottle-vase, Faversham, Kent

these mounds have long disappeared. Cremations would have had much smaller mounds above them.

The sites of many Anglo-Saxon cemeteries were built over long ago, and the burials scattered without record. In other instances the building of a church and the interment of new burials around it destroyed older pagan graves. Even where the old cemetery has never been built on, all surface signs have been destroyed by ploughing. Consequently, although hundreds of Anglo-Saxon burial-grounds have been found and some record made of them in the last 200 years, many more have been lost without trace. But almost every year a new one or two are discovered to add a little more to our knowledge of the earliest English people.

During the first century of the settlement warriors who were killed whilst raiding on the frontiers of the conquered regions were often buried with their weapons in the barrows of earlier peoples. Many of these are known from Wiltshire, Hampshire, and Yorkshire. Sometimes, within the settled regions, a Saxon village would use a Bronze Age barrow for its cemetery, and the dead were placed in a ring round the outer edge of the mound. This arrangement was found at Stanton Harcourt, Oxfordshire, and at Driffield, Yorkshire.

Occasionally, however, a chieftain had a large barrow heaped over his remains, with which were placed his most treasured possessions. One of the best preserved Saxon barrows may be seen in the private grounds of Taplow Court by the Thames in Buckinghamshire. The name of the place includes the name of the chieftain buried there in the early seventh century, and Taplow means, in fact, 'the burial mound of *Taeppa*'.

Even more magnificent was the jewellery and wealth of other objects discovered in a ship burial at Sutton Hoo, just across the river from Woodbridge, Suffolk. Here, in a royal cemetery of eleven barrows, there was at least one other boat-burial, and seven mounds have still to yield up their secrets. The wonderful treasures from both Taplow and Sutton Hoo are in the British Museum. Barrows of apparently similar kind exist at Martlesham, near Ipswich.

Another barrow that yielded interesting information was the one at Asthall, near Burford, Oxfordshire. Although the burial was of about the same time as the one at Taplow, this was a cremation, an unusually late one. With it were two hand-made pots, a jug turned on the wheel, and some fragments of a bronze bowl. This instance proves that the Saxons sometimes cremated their dead long after the custom had gone out of general use. It came to an end entirely after the conversion to Christianity.

In the Jutish kingdom of Kent there remain two grave-yards (out of the many that could still be seen in the nine-teenth century) which can be recognized by surface indica-tions. They exist on Barham and Derringstone Downs, a few miles south-east of Canterbury. On the surface are numerous low burial mounds quite clearly to be seen, though most of them have already been opened. For Lon-doners there is a good example of such a cemetery in Greenwich Park. Its position is marked on the One-Inch map. Excavation in 1784 produced little but traces of wool-len and linen cloth in which the dead had been wrapped. The Kentish cemeteries, on the other hand, almost always included a few graves containing fine jewellery besides the majority which held only a burial without goods.

At Farthingdown, Coulsdon, Surrey, in a Saxon region, sixteen small barrows were excavated in 1873, and in recent years some flat graves were opened. Bucket-like vessels and some weapons and trinkets were found. In the Isle of Wight, which like Kent was settled by the Jutes, the One-Inch map shows the sites of cemeteries on Chessell and Bowcombe Downs. The first of these consisted of flat graves, but on Bowcombe Down an older barrow had been used for the Jutish burials.

Another barrow that is thought to have been made in the Saxon period still exists on Lowbury Hill, Aston Tirrold, Berkshire, where the low mound stands just outside a Romano-British farm enclosure. Another may be seen in a copse on Allington Hill, Bottisham, Cambridgeshire. Others exist at Benty Grange, Derbyshire, and at Burgh le Marsh, Lincolnshire. These are of course in addition to those at Asthall, Taplow, and Sutton Hoo. I know of no other sur-viving Saxon barrows, but there may well be some not yet recognized.

So far I have spoken of nothing but burials, and for the

good reason that very few dwellings have been recognized and excavated. More no doubt will be found, but rather by chance than by deliberate searching. Traces on the surface are likely to be slight. In any case, most Anglo-Saxon villages are covered by modern houses; it is only where they were deserted in early times that we can expect to learn much about the oldest settlements. As, however, 1,300 deserted mediaeval villages have already been recognized, there is hope that some among them will preserve traces of the handiwork of their first founders in Anglo-Saxon times; and there should be opportunities, even for the amateur, to join in the great investigation of these sites which is now beginning.

Another kind of relic of the Dark Ages is the great running earthworks which are to be seen in many counties. Some were made by the Romano-Britons against raiding bands of Angles and Saxons, and others were built by the English tribes as boundary works between their kingdoms. The most famous of the early period is the Wansdyke (map, p. 58, south-west corner and Pl. 13a), almost certainly built by the Britons about A.D. 500 to prevent the Saxons of the Thames valley from spreading southwards. The Dyke runs from Savernake in Wiltshire to the south of Bath. There are detached sections at both the eastern and western ends, which cover openings through forests or the marshy valleys of rivers. From near Bathford, Somerset, to Morgan's Hill near Devizes, the Dyke is built on the *agger* of the main Roman road that led from London to Bath. The Wansdyke was made after the road had lost its purpose and the two towns had lost their occupants.

Bokerly Ditch (map, p. 56 and Pl. 13b), not nearly so long, but as formidable as Wansdyke, was built in the fourth century and was altered on two occasions. It was very likely called into use again to prevent the English settlers round

Salisbury from penetrating to the south-west into Dorset. Situated on the lonely chalk uplands between Salisbury and Blandford, it extends from the British settlement at Wood-yates south-eastwards across Pentridge to the edge of the old forest beyond.

Wansdyke and Bokerly were built by the Britons as a defence against barbarian raiders or against Saxon invaders, but in East Anglia there are several dykes that were almost certainly made by the East Angles or by the Middle Angles to mark a frontier and to hamper cattle-raiding. They were placed across a strip of open country which at its ends joins the Wash to the middle Thames valley. Along it ran the prehistoric trunk route called the Icknield Way, and the dykes were built from the Fens round Cambridge to the thick forests which formed a barrier on the sticky clays of north-western Essex. They are called Bran, Brent, Fleam, and Devil's Ditches, and the last mentioned is a particularly fine example. They saw some savage fighting. Nearly fifty beheaded skeletons were unearthed at the Bran Ditch, some horribly hacked about. Six were found at another section of this ditch; and Saxon weapons have been discovered at the Fleam and Devil's Ditches.

Up and down England there are many known boundary-works of a lesser kind which probably belong to the Saxon period. Those at Froxfield in Hampshire may have been made to mark the division between the South Saxons of Sussex and the *Meonware* of Hampshire, who were Jutes. Similarly, the Grim's Ditches of the Chiltern Hills (best seen near Nuffield, Oxfordshire, and Berkhamsted, Hert-fordshire) (Pl. 15) could have been built to mark a bound-ary between the Saxon settlers in the plain below the Hills and the Romano-Britons of the London region.

Almost everywhere that ancient trackways proceed along the crest of a line of hills you may expect to find very short stretches of 'cross-dykes' barring the track (map, p. 58, north-east corner). They are pre-Roman and may have been toll-points; certainly the local inhabitants could, by means of them, gain control over movement through their territories. Otherwise, apart from the late Bronze Age ranch-boundaries described in Chapter 4, earthworks extending in a line that does not enclose a small area, like a hill-fort, or a larger area, like a ranch-boundary, belong to the Belgic period or later. Belgic earthworks were briefly considered in Chapter 5. But the greatest boundary earthwork of all belongs to a time much later than any so far mentioned. It is Offa's Dyke, which runs for more than 120 miles, with some breaks in remote forested country, from the estuary of the Severn near Chepstow to the estuary of the river Dee near Chester. King Offa of Mercia (757–96) built the dyke as a frontier between his Anglian kingdom of the midlands and the lands of the Welsh. It still runs close to the boundary between England and Wales for most of its length.

A common sight on the downs of southern England are the long terraces keeping roughly to one level, rather like very narrow steps covering a broad hillside. These are called 'strip-lynchets' and represent the narrow fields of Saxon and possibly later farmers. They were probably in use before the rich soils of the valleys had been drained sufficiently to allow crops to be grown on them; and, because strip-lynchets are usually difficult to cultivate, they would not have continued in use once richer and easier fields had been broken by the plough. At three places in Wiltshire and Hampshire Iron Age pottery has been found in the lynchets, and it may be that the Belgae were the first to begin ploughing these slopes. We can be sure, however, that most peasant farming of the Iron Age and Roman periods was by a different method. It produced the small squarish 'Celtic' fields that are still clearly marked by lynchets; and both kinds of lynchets were formed by the same processes (see pp. 98 and 99).

During the struggles with the Danes in the ninth century *burhs* (earthen forts) with a palisade were built by the West Saxon kings, especially Alfred the Great (871–99), to provide strongpoints and places of refuge against the Danish raiders. It is now proved by excavation that the ramparts of Wareham (Dorset) and Cricklade (Wiltshire) had this purpose originally, and that they continued in use later as town walls. Wallingford (Berkshire) may be a third example. Certainly all three places occur in a late ninth-century list of *burhs*, as do Burpham, Sussex, and Lydford, Devon, both of which have surviving ramparts that cut off an area of ground which is protected on its other sides by a river. The *burh* of Hastings may be represented by an earthwork on the East Hill. The actual sites of others, possibly with remaining fragments of ramparts, are still to be found. Two that occur to me are Burton Bradstock, Dorset, and Burton near Christchurch, Hampshire. Both names were originally *burh-tun* (the farm in or by the *burh*), and in such positions, close to rivers, the forts are more likely to be post-Roman than prehistoric. Squarish earthworks by the Avon a mile south of Chippenham, Wiltshire, may represent the winter camp known to have been made by the Danes in A.D. 878.

Possible traces of other Danish forts of the same period can be seen at Hamsterley Castles (Durham); at Castle Rough, Milton (Kent), where many skeletons were found just outside the rampart; at Benfleet, Essex; a fragment at Shoebury, Essex, and a small section at Willington, Bedfordshire. Earthworks at Warham and Holkham, Norfolk, may also be of the same period.

The *burhs* for defence against the Danes were not altogether a new idea. It is likely that most Saxon landowners, even in the earliest centuries, defended their homesteads with a ditch and earthen bank topped with a palisade. No Saxon examples are yet known, though the laws of the earlier kings (of the sixth and seventh centuries) make reference to them. What can be seen in abundance in many counties are the moated sites of the Middle Ages, many of them probably successors to Saxon farmsteads. A glance at a series of One-Inch maps will soon reveal them; and a number of them should be visited and studied so that you may recognize the very many unrecorded examples still to be found. The counties round London, in East Anglia, and on the Welsh Marches, especially Herefordshire, still have many surviving, and quite often they are remote from modern dwellings. This fact, in itself, offers an interesting piece of study for the enthusiast.

The motte-and-bailey castles of the Norman period (map, p. 56, south-east corner) have frequently been much altered even where later mediaeval building has not altogether destroyed the earthworks. Here again new examples are occasionally found, and they offer further opportunities to the keen amateur to make discoveries. Mediaeval park enclosures and deserted villages also await their investigators and, as I have already said, a great new co-operative effort among scholars is beginning for the excavation and study of the villages of which already over 1,300 are known. Certainly no one can say that post-Roman archaeology lacks in interest or opportunity for those who love the open air and are not put off by the thought of muddy boots and a sharpened appetite; they have each the chance to add a few new fragments to our total body of knowledge.

Things to be seen in the Open Air

A wide selection of the many kinds of post-Roman earthworks is given in the chapter.

In Museums

Objects from Anglo-Saxon and Jutish graves, especially in the British and London Museums; in the Ashmolean, Oxford; the Museum of Ethnology and Archaeology, Cambridge; and museums at Lewes, Devizes, Salisbury, Maidstone, Canterbury, Norwich, Guildford, York, and elsewhere.

8: What You Can Do

In the last chapter I offered some suggestions about field work that could be undertaken by anyone ready to do some preliminary planning beforehand. In earlier chapters a number of other suggestions were made which might enable the amateur to add to our sum of knowledge of the distant past. Ever since prehistory became a subject of serious study in this country, amateurs have made great contributions to the subject. Even to-day there are comparatively few full-time professional archaeologists, and there is still a great deal that amateurs can undertake without doing something that has already been done. But, if they are not to be disappointed, they must go about the work in a businesslike way. What follows are some general suggestions that should help in this. They are written with young people in mind who have little money to spare for archaeology.

For most people archaeology is a local matter, confined to districts within easy reach of home. Even the Londoner will find plenty of interest within cycling distance, and he has the advantage of the finest museums and good local libraries. But there are further opportunities for most people when they are on holiday, whether at a sea-side resort or inland in the country. Many of the examples of earthworks that I have chosen in earlier chapters were included because they were near resorts or large towns.

You will need books and maps first of all. Most of the books can be borrowed from the public library, and any book not on the shelves there should be obtainable through the regional library schemes, at a very small cost to you. I mention several of the most useful books in this chapter, and in them you will find references to yet other works which you may consult according to your particular interests. But before you concentrate on any one period of prehistory, or any one kind of ancient monument, you should obtain as wide a knowledge of all periods and monuments as you possibly can.

There is at least one book that you must buy. It is called *Field Archaeology – Some Notes for Beginners issued by the Ordnance Survey*. It is published by Her Majesty's Stationery Office (H.M.S.O., for short) and costs only 2s. 6d. It can be obtained through any bookseller. It describes briefly all the many kinds of field antiquities and gives lists of books for further reading. A chapter on 'Work in the Field', and on how to recognize archaeological sites is especially valuable. You will also find it useful to possess a copy of *Ancient Monuments* for the region in which you intend to do field work. There are six volumes, published by H.M.S.O.: vol. I – *Northern England*; vol. II – *Southern England*; vol. III – *East Anglia and the Midlands*; vol. IV – *South Wales*; vol. V. – *North Wales*; and vol. VI – *Scotland*. These books are well bound, except for volume v, and well illustrated, and they cost only 3s. 6d. or 5s. They begin with an outline of the regional prehistory and mention outstanding monuments that can be visited. Later chapters deal with buildings of the Middle Ages and early modern times, and at the end are very useful notes on the monuments of the region which are in the care of the Ministry of Works.

Besides the local maps that you will need it is as well to have a copy of the Ordnance Survey map of *Ancient Britain*. It is published in two sheets, *North* and *South*, and has as its sub-title: *A Map of the Major Visible Antiquities of Great Britain Older than A.D. 1066*. It is on a scale of about ten miles to one inch and in its most expensive form (backed on linen) costs 7s. 6d. a sheet. The index is most valuable. These maps cannot be borrowed from a library and you will probably wish to refer to them so often that you will need to have copies of your own.

The local maps that you will need should be on as large a scale as you can afford, and certainly not less than one inch to the mile. The larger scales, two and a half inches or six inches to the mile, cover much smaller areas on each sheet, yet they are essential for any special study. If you buy them on paper (not backed with linen) and flat, they cost much less. If you look carefully at a folded copy you can imitate the folds so that it is easy to refer to any part of the sheet without unfurling the whole thing – a dangerous procedure in a high wind on a hill-top. I have found that paper maps, unmounted, last almost as long as the more expensive ones.

The One-Inch map indicates prehistoric, Roman, and mediaeval antiquities in special forms of lettering, and on most of the 190 English and Welsh sheets you are likely to find quite a number of sites to visit. In some regions, Wessex or Dartmoor, for instance, they crowd together in many parts of the map. Visit as many as you can at every opportunity, and get to know them so well that you will easily recognize others of the same kind even if they are not on the map. Before going to any one of them, however, find out all you can about it; and if it has been excavated, read as much as possible of the excavation report, especially the 'Conclusion' (the report should be obtainable through the public library). Some of the 'finds' from the site are likely to be in the local museum. Go and see them, and ask the curator for further information. Most curators are pleased to help anyone who shows real interest in the exhibits. Often, too, they can show you things that have not been put into the glass cases.

You must be gathering experience at every opportunity.

If you can afford it, join the county archaeological society and attend the meetings. As a member you will receive a yearly volume of transactions, some of which make important contributions to knowledge. You will also have the chance to visit ancient sites with other members, and can ask questions on matters that are puzzling. Spend as much time as you can with people who are interested in archaeology and you will gain much.

Right through the spring, summer, and autumn months excavations are going on in almost every county. Amateurs who will cheerfully do as they are asked and who are not unwilling to do heavy work are almost always welcome. There are several good books about methods of excavation, surveying, and recording; but no book can take the place of practical experience. On a 'dig' you will hear many interesting conversations and have opportunities of handling pottery and small finds. If your field work is to be really useful you need to know something about pottery, and one of the best ways of getting to know it is by handling, washing, and sorting it.

As a result of these contacts with archaeologists and of experience, your field work will take on a new and fuller meaning. When you visit a habitation site such as an Iron Age hamlet or hill-fort, or a Roman town or villa-site, make a point of carefully turning over every molehill and rabbit-scrape for pottery. If there is arable near by, inspect that too, but without doing damage to crops. Sometimes dozens of sherds will turn up in a short walk round, but quite often, so I have found, nothing of any kind appears. The most useful sherds for identification are those from a rim or a base, or any piece with decoration on it. For a long time you will have to rely on more experienced people to identify it.

Whenever sewers, cables, or water-pipes are being laid down in town or country, look along the sides of the trench for signs of silted-up ditches showing as a darker patch stretching down from the surface. You may also see the footings of brick or stone walls that have been broken through by the workmen. A careful search along the bank of soil may bring the reward of sherds or even coins if the workmen are not sharp-eyed.

In some parts of the country there are many earthworks, often very slight on the surface, still to be found. Ploughed down barrows, enclosures, hill-forts, Celtic and Saxon field-systems and running earthworks are all still to be discovered in many areas. Record them accurately on the map, preferably the six-inch. If you can return to the spot when the sun is low in the morning or evening, you will see much more of them because of the shadows cast by even the slightest disturbances of the soil. Light snow that has drifted will also help by accumulating even in shallow ditches and on the windward side of banks otherwise invisible. In the Fens very slight flooding of only a few inches deep will show up the patterns of field boundaries, tracks, farmstead sites, and roads. After long drought grass and other crops over silted ditches in any region of Britain will show up the greener, and will dry out or be stunted immediately above wall-foundations.

These sites can, of course, be seen better from the air, but even Air Cadets are unlikely to be airborne in the right place at the right time; and some signs can usually be detected from the ground if the conditions are right. If the site is on a hillside or on one side of a valley and you can climb a facing slope on the other side, you have in fact an airman's view. In this way I have found many Iron Age or Romano-British hamlets that were not marked on the map. It is well to study minutely the many excellent air photographs published in modern books on archaeology. Above all, borrow and study *Wessex from the Air* by O. G. S. Crawford and A. Keiller. They provide diagrams explaining their air photographs that will greatly help you in knowing what to look for. (Figure A on p. 97 is drawn from an air photograph taken when the sun was low. Pls. 1b and 9 were taken in similar conditions.)

If you have a camera with an f.6.3 lens or better, and with several shutter-speeds, you can make a permanent photographic record of your discoveries. Use the fastest film; one famous brand has roll-film with the very high speed of 34° Scheiner, which allows short exposures in poor light. There must usually be some sunshine, and so that banks shall not hide their shadows your camera will have to face almost into the sun. This necessitates a lens-hood, which is in any case advisable at all times. If you can afford an exposure meter, use it always; otherwise follow faithfully the instructions that are given in the form of a leaflet in most film cartons. In poor light long exposures may be necessary, and as it is unlikely that you can hold the camera completely still for more than $\frac{1}{50}$ of a second, a tripod is necessary and a cable-release for the shutter, which will avoid jerking as you expose. If you can't afford these expensive extras, you may still take good photographs of some kinds of site in a normal light; but shadow sites will usually be beyond the power of your camera.

To save money you may develop and print your own photographs. But not every house has a room that can easily be made light-proof. Therefore you will need to go to a chemist to have the job done for you. Have the roll 'fine-grain' developed first of all and only then have prints, or, better still, quarter-plate enlargements made. This avoids paying for prints from poor negatives; once the film has been developed you can choose which are worth printing. Give a serial number to each roll and a separate one to each print from it; enter these, with full details of each exposure, under the appropriate date in your diary immediately after each exposure has been made. A typical note made in the field would read: 'VII, 2; $\frac{1}{5}$ sec.; at f.11; 34° Scheiner; with hood and yellow filter – site at (National Grid reference taken from your map) OR $\frac{3}{4}$ mile N.N.W. West Pelham, 6.45 p.m.' with a note concerning the light. These details should be added in light pencilling on the back of your prints. If you fail to keep a careful record of your prints they will lose much of their value, and you will regret it later because of the muddle they will be in. Two very different earthworks can look very much alike in a small photograph. The purely photographic details are necessary in order to avoid repeating mistakes of exposure. When you have become experienced they may be left out.

When you find anything at all likely to be significant, as for example a sherd, in an area where prehistoric habitation sites would not normally be expected, or a coin, brooch, or flint implement and so on, record the *exact* find-spot immediately. This may lead to the discovery of a new site with the minimum of trouble. There is no surer method of exact location than the National Grid reference obtainable from all the newer Ordnance Survey maps. You will find the system explained on the card cover and at the foot of the maps. Clearly, the next step is to report the find with all details to your local museum. To keep things to yourself will prevent others from extracting all the information possible from your finds. Give them to the museum if the curator will have them; a private collector is not thought well of in these days and can be a great obstacle to the advance of knowledge.

A final word about the clues that may lead to ancient sites. The place-names on your map may start a profitable trail. Names, even of houses or farms, ending in -borough, -bury, -burgh, -burrow, etc., from old English *burh* (fortified place, usually with earth-work), may stand near the site of an earthwork completely destroyed by the plough. Names with -low, -law (from O.E. *hlaw*), or -bury, etc. (from O.E. *beorh*), and tump or toot may give a clue to the site of a lost barrow. Names ending in -chester, -caster, -cester usually preserve the memory of a Roman camp or villa site. Stanchester and Balchester in north Hampshire are both near the remains of villas.

Before you begin searching in the open, look up the name in the county volume of the English Place-name Survey, or, if your county volume is not yet published, in E. Ekwall, *Oxford Dictionary of English Place-Names* which, however, contains few minor names like those of farms. Look for it also in the index of *English Place-Name Elements*, the two volumes of which were published in 1956. It is important to find out whether the name is an old one or merely given by a recent owner. Your local library may be able to help in tracking down the age of the name if all else fails. In my book, *An Archaeology of South-East England*, there is a whole chapter given to the use of place-names in field archaeology.

A site may, however, be found solely through surface indications in the field. A patch of blacker soil in ploughland for instance, should be investigated. If there are sherds, pieces of fired daub or fragments of oyster-shell or Roman brick, it will be worth going over the ground slowly, yard by yard. The best time to look is after heavy rain has rinsed the soil from surface objects. If a watch is kept on a particular field year by year, enough surface material may be picked up to provide a fair indication of the age and nature of the site. It is also necessary to look at neighbouring unploughed areas to find any surviving earthworks that might have been associated with the site. This search also should be made in many different lights and seasons of the year. The best account of methods of searching is to be found in the booklet *Field Archaeology. . . for Beginners* mentioned earlier.

Some readers will not want to go in search of new facts about the past. They will be content to visit sites that are already known and marked on the map. Even this can give much pleasure; but the greatest joy of all is in playing the detective and searching for clues to solve the many mysteries of the past. Those who do this will never find a country walk dull, and their walks will take them increasingly by places where the distant past has left its mark. When out-of-door activity is impossible, there are museums and libraries to be visited and, above all, a good map by the fireside in winter for the planning of new expeditions.

Index

INDEX

INDEX